Typeset by Corinna Downes,
Cover and Layout by Poppypetal for CFZ Communications
Using Microsoft Word 2000, Microsoft , Publisher 2000, Adobe Photoshop CS.

First published in Great Britain by CFZ Press

**CFZ Press
Myrtle Cottage
Woolsery
Bideford
North Devon
EX39 5QR**

© CFZ MMXIII

All rights reserved. Without limiting the rights under copyright reserved above, no part of this publication may be reproduced, stored in or introduced into a retrieval system, or transmitted, in any form of by any means (electronic, mechanical, photocopying, recording or otherwise), without the prior written permission of both the copyright owners and the publishers of this book.

ISBN: 978-1-909488-08-3

AUTHOR'S NOTE

"Mount Pisgah" is an imaginary church name, and all its members appear here under pseudonyms. I have been visiting Spiritual Baptist Churches for over thirty years, and have described a Composite Church in these pages. This is going directly against the spirit of Scientific Folklore, a spirit who demands footnotes, names of informants, addresses, dates and whatnot. Fortunately, I am a spiritual disciple of the Great Zora Neale Hurston and don't need Science to tell me what to do! Read and believe.

Painting on church wall, near altar
(Sketch by Roy Kerridge)

The Spiritual Baptist Church

On New Year's Eve, nineteen ninety three, Bishop Powell of Mount Pisgah Spiritual Baptist Church, breathed his last. I was shocked when I heard the news, as I had known the jovial black-bearded bishop for over ten years. Sometimes known as Pastor or Archbishop, he had been the founder and mainstay of his little church, moving it about here and there all over London before finally settling on a former shop in Harlesden.

Red and green flags outside the little shop proclaim it to be a Spiritual Church, one that specialises in "healing the sick and assisting the demon-possessed." These activities blend into one another, as both occasions call for holy dancing to drum rhythms and the casting out of evil spirits. Bishop Powell's Christianity had an African flavour. However, he and at least half the congregation came from the troubled Caribbean island of Grenada. The other half hailed from various other West Indian islands, with the occasional English or Nigerian visitor. As I write, the church is struggling on without its spiritual leader.

In the early nineteen fifties, many Grenadian islanders emigrated *within* the Caribbean to Trinidad, in search of a better life. Although Trinidad and Grenada were at that time both British possessions whose Negro inhabitants looked alike to outsiders, Grenadans felt nervous and foreign in rumbustious Trinidad. Instead of feeling a "Caribbean oneness", the inhabitants of each West Indian island looked not to a neighbour-island for fellowship, but to the Mother Country, England or France. Anti-Grenadan riots broke out in Trinidad. After a few years of hardships, some of the emigrants moved on to England, and settled in London, Huddersfield, Oxford and Slough. After many vicissitudes, most of the doubly-emigrant found jobs. Wherever they went, they founded little shop-front churches, presided over by Bishop Powell.

A West Indian evangelical pastor is not a mere functionary, like a bad vicar, nor the custodian of a parish, like a good one. He resembles an African village chief. Village chiefs, in most parts of Africa, are well-loved by the villagers and in return feel responsible for them and for the village.

Traditional African villages are sprawling places, the farms and much of the surrounding land under the jurisdiction of one paternalistic Chief. Although Chiefs cannot help having favourites, ideally the well-being of every villager is a Chiefly concern.

Pastors of evangelical churches, throughout the Negro Diaspora from Canada to Cuba, Barbados to both Birminghams (USA and England), resemble Chiefs whose village is their church. In an insecure world, the Pastor is looked to as a central figure in the lives of his flock. A good Pastor is expected to check up on the well-being, spiritual or otherwise, of the flock at all times. He is, or is expected to be, especially concerned when somebody in his church is ill or in any difficulty. If someone does not appear in his customary seat on Sunday, the Pastor is quick to make enquiries. Collections are made in church for members who, the Pastor feels, need money, food or presents. Members speak fondly of "my Pastor." Those who live alone always have someone to call on or someone to visit them. So in my view, a Pastor is a Chief, and the church not mere premises, but a people, a floating village. Churchgoers are often scattered far and wide across a city, and do not (in England at any rate) necessarily live within walking distance of their church building. That is why I call the churchgoers centred on a Pastor-Chief the inhabitants of a floating village.

If a mere Pastor is a Chief, avuncular Bishop Powell must have been a High Chief, a man of great magnificence. Let us visit his church in the days of his splendour, in early nineteen ninety three. Churches in Slough, Oxford and Huddersfield are under his jurisdiction, but at Harlesden's Mount Pisgah he is not only Bishop, but Pastor and Leader. Much of the church ritual has been given to him in dreams, and many of the dreams seem to have been sent from God via African ancestors.

Despite the rows of chrome and plastic tip-up seats, the church resembles a magic cave, the centre pole, a rough-hewn wooden column, adding a grotto-like stalactite touch. This pole, which carries mystic World Tree overtones, obscures the view from the door to the Sanctum at the rear. Once upon a time, only the front room of the shop acted as a church. A wall has been removed at the rear to make room for the pole and Sanctum, the extension heightening the alcove-in-a-cave-of-mystery effect. Candles in multiple holders flicker everywhere, flowers stand in vases or glasses of holy water, and bright murals of Biblical scenes on the walls look as if they have been traced from Victorian children's illustrations. The Sanctum consists of a dais at the far wall, with bannister railings guarding an altar table crowded with bottles of holy oil and water. Bell, book and candle repose here, the bell being a large handbell which the Bishop rings vigorously on occasion, throwing incense around and scattering holy water.

Newcomers are greeted personally by the Bishop in warm booming tones. It is said that all the ladies of the church are in love with him. Robed in thick garments of black or scarlet, like a monk, he usually wears a cloth tied around his head, and carries a thick cord around his neck. Rumour states that he removes this cord at times, to chastise an erring Brother or Sister, yet I have seldom seen him anything but jovial.

Although the only musical instruments in the church, as a rule, are a few tambourines and a bongo drum, the singing is the finest I've heard in a Caribbean congregation. Perhaps this is because there are few teenagers in the church, so the songs are not Americanised into thin reedy pop-gospel. Most of the members are middle-aged women in robes of many colours and white turbans, wooden swords inscribed with holy writing in their Friar Tuck belts. Most of the songs are ordinary hymns from the thin, red Redemption Songbook, mainstay of many an evangelical church. These the Bishop transforms into call and response spirituals, by a technique known as "lining out".

"Abide with me, fast falls the eventide!" he roars, a sing-song solo announcement of a line of verse. The church answers his call by plaintively singing the line, then wait for the next "announcement". Some speculate that this style of singing began in long-ago days when only Pastors knew how to read. Whatever the case, "lining out" transforms a song, not only by making it twice as long, but by calling up a resemblance to a worksong, where a work leader on boat or farm shouts a stylised command which is answered by a chorus.

When the hymn book is put away, the next song might be a "chorus". In "Little Mount Pisgah", the great spirituals of Paul Robeson and Mahalia Jackson are termed "choruses" – rightly so, since all that is retained in each song is the chorus, repeated over and over again, until the rhythm hypnotises and the Holy Spirit descends. Such "choruses" are not learned from records or tapes (if they were, they'd be called "gospel songs"), but apparently evolved in their present form in the Caribbean, perhaps a hundred years ago. Everyday Baptist Sunday School songs are also called "choruses", and so are songs I have only ever heard in Mount Zion.

> "I'm on my way
> To Canaan Land!
> I'm on my way
> To Canaan La-and!
> I've done signed up
> Made up in my mi-ind,
> I'm on my way
> To Canaan Land!
> If my mother-doesn't come
> It won't hinder me-ee,
> If my brother-doesn't –come
> It won't hinder me-ee.
> I've done signed up
> Made up my mi-ind,
> I'm on my way to Canaan Land."

The song is a complete chorus, begun again as soon as it is over. Soon, most of the congregation are on their feet, performing jerky solo dances all over the church. Turbaned women, known as Mothers, lead the way. Privileged Mothers, such as Mother Joy, Fourth Mother of Israel, wear vivid scarlet, with sashes of yellow or blue. One Mother falls to her knees and spins around like a top. Another stands over her, swaying, with palms outspread, as if attempting to mesmerise her or guide her movements. Feebly, I try to jig slightly, to show that I'm taking part in the service.

A tiny round little girl of two stumps over to me and starts laughing merrily.

"You aren't doing it properly!" she says.

Bishop Powell calls a halt by ringing his bell, and his sermon, or "message", begins.

"Greetings to the Household of Faith! Turn to our Bibles, the New Testament, we shall read of Peter in prison."

Everyone turns to the relevant chapter, looking up at the Bishop earnestly. Some twiddle their toes as they turn the pages, for most members remove their shoes, as they sit, and keep them

The Spiritual Baptist Church

under their chairs. As the Bishop reads, adults concentrate but children do not. A small boy gazes up at the portrait of a mysterious white man, Bishop Boltwood, on the wall. Boltwood is said to be the man who ordained Bishop Powell. The boy looks at me, looks at Boltwood, then whispers "Is that you?" I shake my head, fingers on my lips, as the preacher expounds on his subject.

"I have brought God's word to the sufferers in prison!" he booms. "Most of them are innocent, but some are guilty. Sometimes I go to Borstals – awful to hear fifty youths being drilled – 'Left, right! Left, right!' I go many places, but sometimes I travel in Vision, in the Spirit, yes!"

Impressively, he pauses, hangs a bell on a ribbon round his neck, and rings it. In a seat near mine, his mother-in-law, an elfin figure, in her eighties, looks up at her boy with eyes shining in her nutmeg face. When he rings the bell, she gives a little hop, skip and jump, then sits down and adjusts her white headshawl. Everybody calls her Granny Wilkins.

"Yes, in a Vision I was taken up in a high spiritual 'plane, high up, so high! I was in the pilot seat, and God was there behind me, showing me how to steer. As I drove in my spiritual aeroplane, I looked down and saw a broad way, full of people, looking from so high like ants was crawling there. Then I look, an' I see a narrow way, the path to salvation, and it was almost empty! Yes, straight is the gate and narrow the way, if you wants salvation…"

This was not the first time that Bishop Powell had made an involuntary pun, for at one time I used to be puzzled at his constant attacks on socialism, a philosophy which he seemed to equate with voodoo. Finally I realised that he was not being political, but had confused the words "socialism" and "sorcerism". In the end he got it right, and stuck to condemning "sorcerism" – just as well, considering his cordial relations with the local Labour M.P. and councillors. Always good-humoured, the Bishop could laugh at himself, and often did, in between loud condemnation of sinners "outside the church". The doctrine of salvation presupposes a place from which to be saved, and Mount Pisgah-ites are nothing if not apocalyptical. Finally the message ends, and everybody sings.

> "Are you ready? Are you ready?
> Are you ready for the Judgement Day?
> Oh, what a weeping! Oh, what a wailing!
> On that Judgement Day!"

Teacher Sharlene, a big confident teenage girl, still at school, rises to marshal her Sunday School pupils, well-behaved boys and girls aged between four and fourteen. She addresses them in a strong Islington accent, for her home is near "The Cally" (Caledonian Road). 'If a Mother, or a church seer sees a trouble ahead, never be afraid to pray" she admonishes. "I know one little girl here has the blues, 'cos her friends is away in the Caribbean, but God will make sure you see each other again. Are you ready with your song?"

After a false start and some giggling, the children sing one of Teacher Sharlene's favourite

American gospel songs, "You Gotta Move When the Spirit Says Move". She then announces Part Two of the Church Play, the Prodigal Son. With great ease, Teacher Sharlene has tailored the parable into a three-part serial set in modern times. With gusto, the well-rehearsed youngsters throw themselves into their parts.

A dogged-looking ten year old, in a black school jacket, the Prodigal is first seen explaining, in gruff manly tones, the way he has wasted all his father's money until now there's none left. His trendy friends draw back, appalled at having backed so obvious a loser.

"Will you stand by me?" he asks his flighty-looking girlfriend.

"What, when you got no money! You're joking, man!"

With a shrug, the Prodigal makes his way to the Job Centre. Teacher Sharlene is the business-like clerk.

"Yes, we have plenty of vacancies. Would you like to work in a bank?"

"Yeh, that'd be fine."

"I see. Well, how many G.C.S.E.s have you got? Ideally, they require someone with an 'A' level in Business Studies."

"No, I haven't got any of those."

"I see. Well, what qualifications *have* you got?"

"None at all, actually."

"I see, I see. Well, we can't exactly offer you an office job then, can we? What about this job (produces card) working underground, in a type of waterworks?"

"You mean down the sewers?" the Prodigal asks, outraged and taken aback.

"Sewer related, yes", the clerk replies, carefully. "Well, if you don't want that, there's only farm work …"

If ever a play was to prepare a child for the outside world, this play was the play. We next see the boy sweeping away pig mess with a real broom, abused by his employers and grunted at by very small children purporting to be pigs. One of the Prodigal's friends, more loyal than the rest, comes across him sweeping.

"Is that really you? I can't believe it! Sweeping pigs' mess?"

"Yes, that's me", the Prodigal replies, still sweeping and not looking up.

"I can't believe it! You used to be such a trend-setter, and here you are, in a job like this!"

"Well, here I am". (Sweep, sweep, grunt, grunt.)

"To be continued! Class, take a bow! Come on, pigs"" cries Sharlene, at this realistic if not prophetic point.

All the church applauds, and well they might for the well-acted play has brought a grim breath of the outside world to incense-laden Mount Pisgah.

Bishop Powell beams, praises the Teacher and her pupils, and then announces a Healing Altar Call. Someone "raises a chorus", "David Saw the Stone A-Rolling", and the Healing Call begins.

Healing Services form a very important part of Mount Pisgah worship. They sometimes make disquieting viewing for an outsider, since all Mount Pisgah-ites personify illnesses as evil spirits to be danced out of the body, vanquished and banished by sprinklings of holy water.

As if anxious about the world's opinion, the Bishop rings a bell and shouts "They say we do 'obeah' (magic), but we do good 'obeah' for Jesus! Is anybody sick? Brothers and Sisters, don't be backward in coming forward! Jesus is a healer! Amen!"

So saying, the Bishop runs forward, robe flapping, and seems to attack an ill woman who has come forward in some trepidation. Tambourines play softly, and the congregation hum choruses wordlessly. Raising a truncheon covered in holy writing, he seems about to use it, then stops in mid-blow and caresses the air around the woman's head. Quickly seizing his polished handbell, he presses its clapper down all over the sufferer, particularly on her head. Then, with the attitude of someone who has performed a job well done, he anoints her hair with oil and dances with her vigorously. Finally he disengages himself from her, places her hand in that of a waiting Mother as if in an "Excuse-me" waltz, and kneels to pray. Mother and ill-lady dance, and when the latter sinks down exhausted, she is pronounced cured. Possibly the holy dance removes tension and, once over, induces a feeling of swooning relaxation. Certainly, many non-members set great store by the healing powers of Mount Pisgah-ites, and visit the church when they feel poorly.

No one else volunteers to be ill, so the service is drawn to a close, as everyone in the church stands holding hands in a circle around the centre pole and chanting prayers. The Creed, the Twenty Third Psalm, the Lord's Prayer and a final Benediction are all recited. With happy smiles and cries of greeting, the Mothers, Brothers, Sisters, Seers and children settle down for gossip or play. A young girl passes around with a tray of Coca Colas, and home made cakes. Gradually, members drift out into the night in all their finery, some to cars, some to bus stops and some to homes nearby. Some stay the night, for there are beds upstairs and in a back room.

Once, when I called at Mount Pisgah, the Bishop was away ill, and the Healing Service had to go on without him. One of the Mothers, a round-faced lady in black, with a scarlet turban, had been rash enough to confess to having "a touch of 'flu". All the other robed Mothers took this very seriously, and brought the turbaned Mother out to the middle of the floor. A chorus broke out, to drum and tambourine rhythms, and a woman seized a pole and began to spin around, dipping and waving and banging the pole on the ground. A Trinidadian friend once told me that Shango cultists on that island also spin with poles. Shango is the Yoruba (Nigerian) god of thunder. Mount Pisgah pole-spinning and soul-winning is more Christian in character.

> "Jesus on the mainline, tell Him what you wa-a-ant,
> Tell Him what you want right now!
> Some ask for pa-a-ardon,
> Some ask for peace,
> Some ask for pa-a-ardon
> And kneel at Jesus' feet."

Robes flapped as the Mothers danced round their ill colleague, expressions and gestures charged with vehemence and extreme ferocity. Those evil spirits had better look out! The rhythm grew choppy, the words of the song lost coherence, and the glaring dancers jerked and jack-knifed their bodies. A sunwheel of candles, fixed halfway up the centre pole, was spun by tugging a maypole ribbon until it seemed a circle of flame. In a semi-trance, the ill Mother danced with a glittering-eyed old lady who began a frightening snorting song, uttered in "tongues" with great intensity. Face to face they danced, with hunched shoulders, the singer fierce, the ill Mother uneasy and afraid.

> "Huh! Hurdle!
> Huh! Hakkada!
> Huh! Hurdle!
> Huh! Hakkada!"

The Mother staggered, as others joined in the song, interspersing the "Hurdles" with loud menacing whoops. Little girls left their parents and took up the dance, one poking her tongue out at a friend. Truncheons inscribed with spirit-writing sawed the air like fiddlesticks. Swaying and groaning, the ill woman fell into a chair, where she lolled as if in a faint.

"Go on dancing everyone", the glittering-eyed lady ordered sharply. Then she addressed the evil spirits inside the ill woman. "Come out! Come out!"

Someone ran for a basin, and the ill woman began to vomit. The pole spun, the change continued.

"I feel better now", the ill woman declared feebly.

At once the "hurdling" stopped, as the presiding Mother ran to open the door to the street, and to bang it three times.

"Did anyone see anything?" she asked breathlessly.
"To be honest, I didn't see anything, but I felt it," someone said.

"Yes, I think it ran out of the door," another agreed.

"Ha! Some people think they get 'flu and something else follow!"

"Yes, they get possessed!" one of the women exclaimed.

Once the sufferer had been led to a back room, the service went on, with a short Message from the absent Bishop's wife, Mother Jewel. She was his third wife. When they had married a few years earlier, Mother Jewel had been a sprightly girl of pixyish beauty. Now, agitated by her husband's illness, she seemed distraught, angry and almost apoplectic. A fiery-eyed woman in scarlet robes.

"Greetings to the Household of Faith! We must pray for all the children of the church. Some are of an age when they can turn Rasta! If we do not pray, Satan may allow some of the little ones to become ill. It is a time of year for coughs and sneezes. Nothing has been right since the scientists made a space shuttle to spy on Heaven!"

"Ha!" several women cried, in bitter triumph over the folly of scientists.

"When Man went to the moon, all kind of 'flu and diseases follow!"

There was a chorus of "True, ah, true", and the speaker continued.

"Children! Kneel and pray!"

Obediently, all the youngsters kneeled on the floor in a row, Mohammedan style. After lengthy prayers, they were allowed to return to their seats, looking subdued. Mother Jewel, afraid that her husband might never recover, called forth a visiting pastor, a serious-looking man in black robes and a red bandana.

"Pray! Pray for us all in little Mount Pisgah!"

The pastor in black began to pray in a sing-song voice, as soft music broke out anew, followed by another song.

> "The hand of God is on the wall!
> The hand of God is on the wall!
> The hand of God is on the wa-a-all,
> You can see the writing on the wall!"

Evidently, the stand-in pastor's praying did not please Mother Jewel at all.

"You are not getting out the word on your heart!" she accused him.

Ever practical, the formidable Mother seized the hapless man in both hands, and began to press his heart and back, moving her hands upwards towards his throat. She was squeezing the words on his heart upward towards his mouth. Struggling together, the two of them hummed and jerked to the music, the choking pastor a puppet in her hands. A croak came out, but no "word", and the Mother released him in scorn.

"He has no word on his heart! Ha! It is not enough for a man to be called a Leader – he must *be* a Leader, and be uncomplaining."

So saying, Mother Jewel removed her thick rope necklace and began to beat the pastor with it, gently at first, then with increasing vigour, but never enough to hurt him. All this while, I had been looking around for Mother Jewel's mother, Granny Wilkins. Granny Wilkins idolised Bishop Powell, and was idolised herself by the church children. Her presence usually had a softening effect on Mount Pisgah. But she was nowhere to be seen.

Just as I was wondering if I had become possessed myself, the door burst open and little Granny Wilkins danced and skipped into the centre of the room, in the attitude of a nymph scattering flowers before the entrance of the Goddess of Spring. Her brown eyes shone mischievously.

"Praise the Lord! Praise the Lord!" she carolled.

Close behind her appeared not the Goddess of Spring, but Bishop Powell himself, shuffling slowly along wrapped from head to foot in a blanket, a walking stick in one hand. He seemed to have aged forty years overnight. As he tottered along, he sang in a surprisingly strong and melodious voice.

> "I'm coming! I'm coming! My head is bending low;
> I hear the angel voices calling
> 'Old Black Joe'."

Everyone stared, stunned. Having reached the centre pole, with one more cry of "Old Black Joe", Bishop Powell hurled stick and blanket to the ground and stood triumphantly in his finest robes, apparently perfectly well! He had made a miraculous recovery, and stood with arms outspread, laughing heartily at the practical joke he and Granny Wilkins had played on the flock. A warm spirit of laughter filled the church, the pastor in black cast a look at Heaven that said "Saved by the bell!" and the Bishop gracefully took over the service from Mother Jewel.

A little later, I hurried home, the strains of an eerie chant running through my head.

The Spiritual Baptist Church

"Huh! Hurdle!
Huh! Hakkada!"

Every August, Mount Pisgah and other Spiritual Baptist Churches hold a sea baptism at a selected resort. Non-members buy tickets at the church, and come along for a day at the seaside. Coaches pick up passengers, church members and baptismal candidates from various parts of West Indianised Britain.

In July, a few weeks before the great coach outing, Mount Pisgah and its brother churches hold Conventions, packed week-long meetings in which the converts are prepared for their ordeal by sea water. So arduous are the preparations for baptism, that they resemble initiation rites for warriors of an unusually hardy forest tribe. No one actually mutilates the candidates, or places killer ants on their bodies, but there is plenty of marching on the spot, or enforced jerky dancing, together with sergeant-majorish abuse from senior church officers or Warrior Shepherds.

On my first visit to Mount Pisgah Convention, I found all five candidates sitting in the front row, directly below the altar, a place known as the Mercy Seat. Two were young women, one was a stout middle-aged woman, one a simpering man of thirty with a shock of "Afro-fuzzy" hair and the last a timid elderly man whose bald head was beaded with sweat. His wife, a robed Mother of long-standing in Mount Pisgah, sat triumphantly behind him. As I entered, she was praying aloud, in a sing-song voice.

"I'm kneeling at the Mercy Seat
Where Jesus answers prayer."

A robust Mother appeared from a side door, bearing a basin of warm water, towels over her arm. Already barefoot, their shoes beneath their seats, the candidates prepared for Feetwashing, an important part of pre-baptismal purification. Bishop Powell and a team of Mothers kneeled in a row together and swabbed at dark feet dangling in a succession of basins. Tenderly, with flannels, they obeyed St. Peter's injunction: "Lord, not my feel only, but also my hands and my head." I could almost feel the relief of the bald-headed man when a wet flannel passed gently over his sweating dome. But his relief was to be short-lived. No sooner had his head been swabbed than Bishop Powell turned on him aggressively and said:

"I know all about *you*! You think you are a Christian! Ha! You have a lot to learn. Now comes the candidates' examination! Do you believe Jesus is the Son of God?"

The poor man quailed and whispered something. Then Bishop Powell turned to the Afro man, a candidate who resembled a 'seventies soul singer, with his floppy white robe, moustache and black halo of hair. Apparently affected by the Holy Spirit, the young man jogged repetitively to the music in his head, uttering grunts and clicks in time with his movements. Now the Bishop's scowl changed to a beam, his harsh voice to the cooing of a dove.

"I know you believe, I don't need to ask", he said. "Brethren, I am greatly pleased by this

Brother! My son, you have the makings of a great priest, and you shall soon have your own church when you return to the Caribbean. I can tell the Household of Faith that I predict a great future for this man!"

Smiling blissfully, his eyes closed, the fortunate candidate jogged, giggled and clicked fervently. Later that evening, he was given real music to jog by. Eyes turned to the door as tall imposing Brother Ricky entered, clad in short-sleeved white robes, his drum around his neck. This was my first encounter with Brother Ricky, but everyone else greeted him as an old friend.

"I love the drum, so I love the drummer man!" Bishop Powell greeted him warmly.

The drummer man, smiling fiercely through his priest-like beard, cast expressive pale grey eyes around the church, a glance of dreamy yet faintly sardonic pride. His young wife, who stood behind him clad in a long dress and a head-bandana, seemed conscious of being the partner of a celebrity. Brother Ricky's drum, one of several he possessed, seemed half-military, half African, with its ribbed framework and blue netting. It had been thickly painted in red and green. Settling down on a chair, drum between his knees, the musician coaxed loud rhythms from his instrument, using his palm and a hand-carved hooked drumstick alternately. I had seen similar hooked drumsticks used by Yoruba experts on the Nigerian speaking-drum.

"Zion wanderer come home!" said Brother Ricky in soft calypsonian tones.

"Sing 'This Train'", a Sister suggested, after a while.

"This Train is bound for Zion, this train…"

No one else knew the words, so the church hummed, murmured and harmonised along, "Bim Bam … a-Bim Bam Bam, This Train!"

Before long, the Convention had become a holy dance, and the bald-headed convert was able to forget his troubles. Sometimes sharp, sometimes booming, Brother Ricky's drumming delighted the church and probably intrigued passers-by several streets away.

"When you're married to Jesus, I'll be there!" he sang.

By midnight, Brother Ricky himself was leading the dancers round and round, swaying, drum-beating and singing.

> "I am the Holy Ghost!
> Remember me!
> I am the Holy Ghost!
> Remember me!
> I am the Prophet Jonah!
> Remember me!"

Night by night, the Mount Pisgah Convention and preparation of candidates continued. The elderly bald-headed man, whose name was Brother Cedric, continued to get into trouble. On one occasion, the terrified church thought they'd killed him. After being questioned by Bishop Powell, prayed over by Mother Jewel and drummed over by Brother Ricky, the poor man fell into a swoon. Pleased at first at such evidence of holiness and repentance, the church danced and sang around his recumbent form.

> "Sow the precious seed!
> Sow the precious seed!
> Harvest Time is coming bye and bye!"

Time passed, but Brother Cedric didn't move a muscle. Brother Ricky struck up a different tune, Mother Jewel laid a wooden cross over the body, but still Brother Cedric wouldn't come round. The atmosphere grew tense.

> "Mary and Martha, gather at the Cross!
> Mary and Martha, gather at the Cross!
> All those who love Jesus gather at the Cross!"

Still Brother Cedric wouldn't move, and the church exchanged panic-stricken glances. ("Somebody help me!" called Mother Jewel). All of a sudden, in one swift movement, Brother Cedric leaped to his feet, one arm raised on high, and cried "I have seen Glory!"

Everyone was intensely relieved, smiles broke out and so did a new song.

> "Never get weary yet!
> Never get weary yet!
> Long long years a-walking in the wilderness
> And I never get weary yet!"

Looking exhausted, Brother Cedric now sank into a seat, Sisters vying with one another to wipe away his sweat. The poor man looked drained and old, and turned piteous eyes to the boisterous figure of Bishop Powell. Unmoved, the Bishop ordered him to open his Bible for a fresh examination. Brother Cedric fumbled, the holy book almost too heavy for him to lift.

"What kind of Christian are you if you can't even open a Bible?" the Bishop roared.

Meanwhile, in other Spiritual Baptist churches, similar preparation of baptismal candidates were taking place. I decided to cross London to Walthamstow in the Far North East, and pay a visit to Mount Ararat, Mount Pisgah's sister church.

The Spiritual Baptist Church

I soon found the newly acquired hall, nestling beside a railway bridge, a large yellow cross fixed over the shed-like door. A worried, white-robed pastor with a small black beard greeted me and showed me to a seat. Whom should I see but Brother Ricky with a conga drum! He gave a surprised cry of recognition and stretched out a long arm to shake my hand. This was his home church, for he was an infrequent visitor to Mount Pisgah.

Taking my seat in the row of chairs behind the Mercy Seat, I took a look around. The newly-acquired hall was bright and whitewashed, with an altar at the far end, but no centre roof pole, or "tree of life". That place was taken by a circular table covered with a white cloth, a broomhandle size pole standing upright in the centre. On top of the pole, flags of every colour radiated in a spin-around circle, resembling a backyard rack for drying washing.

Below the flags on the table stood the usual holy items of a Spiritual Baptist Church. There were dishes of oil, small vases full of laurel leaves or yellow flowers in holy water, burning night-lights, extra glasses of water, a Lota or golden globe, and bottles of olive oil. A polished coconut shell had been intricately carved with patterns, small pictures and the legend "God is Love". Two tall dry palm fronds stood erect beside the table-pole, and a small palm tree sprouted from a pot on the floor. (Palm leaves are sacred in some parts of West Africa). Away up on the altar, looking very Biblical, a seven headed candelabra and seven separate candlesticks burned brightly. Most of the congregation wore white robes, sometimes trimmed with blue or brown. Two of the Sisters in charge were gigantic robed and head-wrapped women, who gave the three candidates a sergeant-majorish hard time.

Side by side, the three candidates for baptism marked time on the spot, arms swinging like pistons and hands held out before them as if in a cup-like plea for alms. Sometimes they were allowed to sit down, but still had to tramp their feet up and down on the floor. As they moved, they all chanted "A-B! A-B!" in rehearsed, mechanical tones. This strict discipline, kept up all night as baptising-day neared, was supposed to break down their outer selves and by means of fainting-fits, visions and sheer exhaustion, bring them nearer to God.

From left to right, the candidates were addressed by their ruthless trainers as Number One, Number Two and Number Three. One and Two were young women in robes, Number Three a young man in ordinary clothes. He was a latecomer, and was not allowed to forget it. One of the two huge Warrior Shepherdesses drilled the hapless candidates.

"Number One! You're just saying 'A-B, A-B' like natural talk! You must reach up, from below your throat, and get the Duption! Like this 'A-hyurp! B-hyurp!' Get the Duption!"

(By the word "hyurp", I mean to indicate a heaving, croaking gasp, sounding as if it emanates from the whole body. Such a convulsive sound helps to encourage possession by angel-spirits. The feeling of imminent possession is called "Duption", a term I have never heard outside Mount Ararat. All three candidates strove hard for the Duption).

"Number Two!" roared the Shepherdess. "Keep tromping! Keep tromping! This is not a game, you know! I'm sorry to have to talk to you like this, but I get so upset if it's not done right! Number Three – swing your arms! You're supposed to be marching and begging for supplication! Keep tromping! Number Two! You are supposed to be tromping, not doing the Bogle, the Butterfly or the Donkey! You are not at Dougie's or the Mezza! (These are night clubs in Hackney where patrons enjoy secular dances, such as the Bogle and Butterfly). Get the Duption! Move your arms! Tromp! When I prepare for me own baptism, I tromp all night from ten until four in the morning! Tromp! I'm almost sorry for you, you know", she added insincerely.

Forcing themselves on, the three candidates desperately tromped, swung and urged on the Duption. Everyone else swayed in more relaxed style to Brother Ricky's drumming. Suddenly a turbaned Mother leaped from her seat, groaned and danced to the round table, where she seized red, yellow and white flowers and strewed their petals like confetti. Filled with Duption, she rang towards Number Three, the male candidate, and butted him repeatedly in the chest. Then she led him out onto the floor and danced with him. Reaching for his hands from behind her back, she seized him and swung him up onto her back like a sack of coal. Triumphantly she carried him around the church, to the admiration of all, as Brother Ricky's drums beat on. Then she put him down, waltzed him around and swung him up on her back once more. As she staggered around with her heavy load, Brother Ricky began to sing,

> "Gonna lay my burden
> Down By the Riverside!
> Down By the Riverside!
> Down By the Riverside!
> Aint gonna carry it away!
> Don't carry it away – don't carry it away!
> I Aint Gonna Carry it Away!"

Well, if that isn't Duption, I don't know what is! Not long after that, there was a short Testimony Service, Church Announcements and then the service broke up with friendly gossip.

"Some people think they are superior to others!" the gigantic Shepherdess testified. "At work, the high-ups walk with their heads up, so proud, they don't speak to me at all. But me, although they are high up and I am a Care Attendant, I walk tall and proud too, and don't speak to them! Ha!"

I felt very sorry for the frail old people Care-Attended by the proud Shepherdess and the "high-ups" in a council home for the elderly.

However, the three candidates seemed so merry and relieved to be released from the thralls of Duption that a pleasant atmosphere prevailed. Soft drinks were produced from a back room, paper cups filled and children began to play.

The Spiritual Baptist Church

A few weeks later, quite by chance, I met a prominent member of the Spiritual Baptist Church of Trinidad, the home country of the faith. Her name was Mother Thelma, a bold or "facedy" forty year old, stocky, forceful and high-spirited in every sense

"Come to my house one evening, and I'll tell you about the *real* Spiritual Baptist Church!" she insisted. "I went to Mount Pisgah, and when I saw what Bishop Powell had done to the church, I was shocked! You see, here everyone is mixed up, from all over the West Indies and Africa! What Bishop Powell has done is mix in other doctrines, like Revival Zion of Jamaica, Jamaican Pentecostalism, Nigerian worship and Grenadan ideas! He should have stuck to proper Trinidadian Spiritual Baptism! Everything they do at Mount Pisgah is wrong! Here's my address – it's near East Ham Tube Station! I'll tell you everything, except some things that are secrets, of course."

Mother Thelma's house turned out to be one of a well-kept row of Victorian terraced villas, in a leafy backwater beside a railway line. Her gum-chewing teenage daughter answered the door and yelled "Mum!" up the stairs.

Soon I was sitting in a modern, airy front-room-with-middle-wall-taken-away, talking to Mother Thelma. Far from being dressed in robes and turban, the Mother wore jeans and a "black Pride" T-shirt.

"If only you could see Trinidad!" she enthused, eyes sparkling with patriotism. "If I ever win the Lottery, I'll take you there! My family in Trinidad come from Nigeria – Yoruba, I mean – and the Congo! We have traditions in our family from both those countries, from my grandparents, and they've been confirmed by my dreams. I've also got cousins in Venezuela. Jimmy, my husband, is a builder – he's out at work now."

The daughter padded in with tea, accompanied by a little brother and sister, whom Thelma briskly shooed away. When they had gone upstairs, my hostess began to talk.

"In Trinidad, we Spiritual Baptists are often called 'Shouter Baptists', while others call us 'Dippers' or 'Shango Baptists.' 'Shango Baptists' indeed! Shango's quite different from us. Because the authorities once frowned on us, we held our meetings right out in the bush, or jungle. I come from the country, in South Trinidad, so I don't know what the churches are like in the city, Port of Spain.

"Here in London, Jamaicans have changed the Spiritual Baptist Church! People call the head of a church 'Pastor', instead of 'Leader', and they even speak in tongues, Pentecostal-style, which comes from the Tower of Babel. Tongues are not a gift of God, they're a punishment from God. I don't regard everything in the Bible as the word of God – some is and some isn't. In Trinidad there are more young people in the church than over here.

"No-one carries batons, or truncheons, in church like Bishop Powell does. We keep feasts and we have pilgrimages, which you never see in London.

The Spiritual Baptist Church

"What are pilgrimages? Well, suppose I came to your church, I might say, 'Brother Roy, next week we shall make a pilgrimage to see you.' So you would get ready, 'cos that means our *whole* church would come, gorgeously dressed in robes, with green or white sashes, playing music and parading along the street from our church to yours. Your church would come out to meet us, and ask us questions, such as 'Where you come from?' and we would reply to each question. Then our two churches would exchange gifts, and every gift would signify something. Again questions would be asked out loud in the street. 'What you giving me this bell for?' or whatever it was, and the giver would have to know how to reply. Then we would sweep in, singing, and just take over your church. Another time, you would make a pilgrimage to us."

Mother Thelma's description reminded me of accounts I've heard of the Masquerades held in West Africa by believers in the old gods. Masked figures in musical processions pause to ask ritual questions and receive ritual-replies from the people that they meet.

"There is a reason behind everything you see in a Spiritual Baptist Church. If you ring the bell nine, seven or five times, each ring has a meaning. The amount of pockets in an apron means something. In Trinidad, when we have a baptising, all the candidates are dressed in blue, and their bands are sealed."

"Meaning?"

"Oh, yes – meaning that the blindfolds, or bands, have spirit-writing on them. We call blindfolds 'bands', and spirit-writing is called 'sealing'. When a member is baptised, he or she is given a secret Word, and that personal Word must never be forgotten. Sometimes a Pundit gets invited, from a Hindu temple, to have a sit-down chant and do the Ramine. When he's finished the Ramine chant, the Pundit will go, and we carry on. Some Spiritual Baptists know the Ramine, and chant on the beach after baptism. There are lots of Indians in Trinidad, and our cooking and religion gets affected by this. I often go to mosques back home, 'cos no one religion knows everything."

I wondered if 'the Ramine' meant 'the Ramayana', a recital of Hindu sacred legend popular among Indians in London, and everywhere else for that matter.

Taking a deep breath, I gave Mother Thelma a significant look and asked, "What is the Duption?"

She gave a start, returned my look and said "Duption!" Shouting is Duption."

"How do you mean?"

Now it was her turn to take a deep breath, as she launched into a description of the Mo'ning or Mourning Room behind a door behind the scenes in all Spiritual Baptist Churches. This differed from the Morning Room where my grandparents breakfasted in their Wembley home, and more closely resembled a West African place of initiation into a secret society.

"You must have heard baptismal candidates learning how to sing from down here, below the chest, with exercises, A-B, A-B? No white person could ever withstand these exercises, and the lengthy fasting that goes with them. Not only candidates for baptism, but for all the holy ranks of Spiritual Baptist must undergo these tests and mournings. There are Mothers, Warriors, Shepherdesses, Stargazers, all different. Not till you've had your first mourning can you freely go in and out of the Mourning Room.

"When I first took the t'rone (throne) I was a Young Mother, or First Mother, or Green Mother. I was not a Crowned Mother like my friend Matron Claudette – a Matron is a Second Mother. Now Matron Claudette's job was to clean the church, back in Trinidad. For many years she would mix cow manure and mud together, and 'leapay' the church. You see, our church floor was just ground, and Matron Claudette would spread the mixture and let it harden – we call that 'leapay'. Mourning would go on for seven days and seven nights, with flour bags laid down for visitors to sleep on. But mourners would sleep with the earth as a bed and a rock for a pillow.

" 'Pointing' is the beginning of mourning. Mother Pointers would point you the way how to do things, how to write 'seals', our holy writing. When my spiritual mother pointed me, she had on different bands each day- blindfolds, I mean. During the mourning, spirits come to teach you things. People say 'Have you met the Duption Man?' You mourn and fast, and you've got to meet the Duption Man."

"Have you met the Duption Man?'

"Yes", she replied, after a pause.

"Who is he?"

(Silence).

"Is he natural, or is he a spirit?"

"A spirit. Don't ask me more. All through the mourning, a Nurse is supposed to track you. She can read your mind, she knows your dreams and she can guide you into having the right dreams. My Nurse, Mother Bernadette, knew my dream and told it back to me, about a boat and a 'plane.
"After mourning comes the Proving Night. You have to answer questions and prove that you really did make all your spirit-journeys. There is a song, 'Where are you bound for?' You must leave your body while mourning and fly to Persia, India, Jerusalem, China and at last to Africa. But people pretend, you know! Some never get Duption, never go to Africa, but make out they do. These ones get found out at Proving Night – they try to describe Africa and get it wrong.

"On Proving Night, the Warrior never prompt you, you got to know what to say. When you talk 'in the spirit' and 'come round' afterwards, you should not be able to remember what you said. If you *can* remember, you were not in the spirit, and you get found out on Proving Night. Some things you can prove by remembering, but other things you prove by *not* remembering what you did or said. You would be surprised how many people can't hear the spirits, and try and pretend!"

"No I wouldn't, because that's what I would have to do, if I were there," I explained.

Mother Thelma seemed to feel that she had told me too much already. While she heated up some supper, I reflected on her words. Some of the experiences of mourning-room initiates reminded me of tales I had heard of Roman Catholic Seers at shrines where the Virgin Mary makes visitations. The Seeress of Canvey Island told me that the Virgin possessed her, spoke "below the chest" and that afterwards she (the Seeress) did not know what had been said. Spirit-visits to Africa seemed to be taken for granted by Mother Thelma. Had such mystic visits begun in the days of slavery in Trinidad? Those who knew Africa at first hand might have found consolation in dreams and spirit journeys to the lost Motherland. Perhaps one or two slaves on a sugar plantation might have grown expert in shamanic journeys, and held their fellow captives enthralled by tales of nightly travels. Sometimes they might have been challenged to prove their words. It is known that Trinidadian slaves seldom slept, but stole forth at night to a secret world where humble folk held strange high and mighty titles, just as in Lodge Houses or Spiritual Baptist Churches.

Over my bowl of delicious hot dumplings in dahl soup, I listened enthralled myself, as Mother Thelma told me of her other church, one that alternated with her Spiritual Baptist duties – Orisha.

Orishas are the gods of the Yoruba people, called down by drumbeats to possess initiates. In the New World, the "Orisha religion" is only lightly touched by Christianity and Indian religions. (Indentured labourers from India arrived in the Caribbean after Emancipation, to cut the sugar cane and take the place of slaves).

"I thought Orisha was in Venezuela, not Trinidad", I said, surprised.

"No, we have it too. I go back regularly to attend Orisha ceremonies. Last time, we went real, real deep in the bush, to a tiny clearing right in the middle of the forest, at dead of night, and there was a white man there! (She seemed indignant). He was an American, writing a book. While the drummers played, he made notes, but when the Orisha spirits came down, he put his pen away. Afterwards he sat talking to the drummers as if nothing had happened. Before you go, would you like to see my Orisha shrine?"

To my surprise, I found that a collection of shelves and ornaments in a far corner of the room was actually an Orisha shrine, the first I had ever seen. Above the assorted candles and sea shells, a sugary Indian portrait of Lakshmi the Hindu fortune-goddess smiled at me. A scroll, stretched across the shrine, was "sealed" in the mystic symbols I had seen so often in Mount Pisgah Spiritual Baptist Church. Beside these pictograms, a list of major Orishas, in very small English writing, captured my attention. It was headed by the name "Olorun", the

Yoruba word for "God", "Great Spirit", or "Creator". Among the names on the list I recognised that of Ogun, Yoruba god of war and iron, whose sacrifice is a dog. A big, stout, twisty pole leaned against the wall, the bark peeling off in patches.

"This is a very good staff – it was given to me at my first ceremony", said Mother Thelma. She picked it up, held it proudly for a moment, then showed me a large bamboo hoop, handled with the utmost reverence.

"This hoop is called 'Peso', and the Orishas come down and go through it", I was told. Bound by oaths, Mother Thelma could tell me no more. So I thanked her for a lovely evening and went home.

Had I met Mother Thelma at a school gate or in a shop, I would have thought her to be a modern-minded Strong Woman, full not of Duption but of fashionable "black consciousness". As it was, I walked fearfully home through darkened East End streets, looking over my shoulder, and dodging the Duption Man.

At midnight, on the eve of the great sea baptism, the grotto-like church of Mount Pisgah was crowded. Bishop Powell was in fine form, bluff and jovial. Brother Cedric was now in favour, thanks to his spectacular fainting fit. His wife, a black veil over her face, fanned him tenderly.

"I'm so happy that my dear husband came forward at last to seek baptism", she announced proudly.

Brother Ricky was there, tap-tapping on his drum and looking more worldly than ever. Some Sisters looked at him slightly askance, for he wore a T-shirt decorated with a picture of a scarlet devil holding a pitchfork. "I'm a Forking Trinidadian", the legend ran. Bishop Powell looked at him benignly, and then prepared to blindfold the candidates, white cloths hung over one arm. Afro-hair, still out of his mind, was the first to have his eyes bound. Candidates would have to dance blindfolded all night, remain sightless in the coach to the seaside and only recover the use of their eyes when dipped "in Jordan stream".

In order to justify this strange custom, Bishop Powell ordered the church to open their Bibles and read about the Resurrection of Jesus.

"You know the napkin left folded in the tomb?" he queried. "That napkin was the same as the blindfold cloths you see today. When a candidate is blindfolded, it concentrates his mind on prayer! This is Mount Pisgah, and we must do things properly! Some preachers, when they dip, hold the candidate's nose. Or else they make the candidates hold their own noses, so! (Laughter). But this is Mount Pisgah and we don't fool around! Everyone must be properly dressed! You know, when a woman wears trousers, it is an abomination to the Lord! Men should wear trousers, and women wear dresses until the end of time! Yes! My own daughter, now left home an' married, walk around wearing trousers! I am shocked! Say 'Amen', church. And yet, when she was young, I brought her up so well! If I ever see her unruly on the street, I would beat her to the ground!"

When all five candidates were heavily blindfolded, they were each given a burning candle to hold. Then Brother Ricky danced to his feet and began to play his drums in earnest. Soon almost the whole church was dancing, as the Forking Trinidadian played and sang.

> "Samson told Elijah,
> 'Pray the power down!
> Pray for fire and also pray for rain.
> Pray to God
> To help my dying soul.
> I just want to hear Elijah pray again!' "

Unlike the fervent Mount Pisgah-ites, I did not wish to dance all night, so I tiptoed out and hurried home for a good rest before Baptism Day.

Meanwhile, though I didn't know at the time, there had been high drama at Mount Ararat. One of the three candidates, tired of Duption, tromping and eternal insults, had resigned. Later, she told me herself what had happened. A slim girl, with aquiline features, her eyes blazed as she indignantly recalled her treatment at the hands of the seargeant-majorish Shepherdess, whom she referred to as "Mother Persecutor".

"I stood up and I testified – I said 'I am not going to be baptised! Just to make sure, I am going away on holiday on that very day! I have suffered persecution', and with that I looked Mother Persecutor right in the eye! 'I was tromping and tromping', I told her, 'and with every tromp your ears should have been ringing, I was hating you so much! What right have you to speak to me like you have been doing?' I said. 'You don't know me, you don't know my heart and you don't know my God, so why should you criticise me? My God is a merciful God. Why He wants me to be a Spiritual Baptist, I don't know! I am from Brixton, not from Trinidad. Yet every time I pray, He tells me 'Go back to church'. But it may be He don't mean a Spiritual Baptist church! So I wont' be baptised. Why should I change so much, and wear a turban and gown? I've changed too much already.' And with that I sat down."

"Whatever did they say?" I asked, over-awed by her courage and audacity.

"Hmm! Mother Persecutor began to sing, and the others sort of laughed softly and foolishly. Then Pastor stood up and said, 'I know you will be there on the day to be baptised. You see', he said 'God and the Devil often side by side, as in the Book of Job, so when you think you hear the voice of God you is really hearing the voice of Satan! Satan tells you not be baptised', he said. That was the crowning insult, to make out I couldn't tell God from Satan!

I didn't say a word, I just picked up my coat and swept out!"

So it was, that on the sunny morning of the Baptism Day, the combined forces of Mount Pisgah and Mount Ararat could muster only seven candidates. Instead of repining, they made a song out of it, a soulful chant that I could hear as I neared the open doorway of Mount Pisgah.

"Thank God for seven, Lord!
Thank you, Lord, for the seven!"

Buxom Sister Sharlene went bustling about, in and out of the church, carrying bags of fizzy drinks, boxes of candles and armfuls of holy staffs, rods and crosses. Children ran around happily, getting under people's feet. Brightly gowned and aproned Mothers looked up and down the road outside, to see if the coaches were coming. Friends and relatives, unconnected with the church, had bought tickets from Mother Jewel and looked on the event as a holiday coach excursion, the songs and baptisms an extra bonus.

At the back of the church, behind the centre pole, Brother Ricky beat his Yoruba drum, and the candidates danced, blindfolded, while Bishop Powell, his wife and other Mothers sang passionately.

"He touched my finger with a golden pen,
A golden pen, a golden pen!
He touched my finger with a golden pen
And signed my name up there!

Signed my na-a-ame,
He signed my name up there!
He touched my finger with a golden pen
And signed my name up there!"

The song appeared to be very important. I wonder if "heart" had been used instead of finger at one time, as the song would have made more sense that way. The first verse had a jerky rhythm, the second verse was sweetly drawn out and melodic. Since the blindfolded dancers, who appeared to be mesmerised, clutched lighted candles in posies of flowers, they had to be guided in their movements by robed women known as Mount Pisgah Nurses.

In the midst of the music and preparations, an earnest young man came in from the street and asked if he could use a photo-copy machine to duplicate a tract he had written, a message from God sent in a dream. Several Mothers stopped to read the tract with interest, and a young woman said that she would photo-copy it at her work, as the church had no machine.

Mystic chalk drawing on the carpet, carried out vigorously during the service, rubbed out later. "What does it mean? That's a secret.'

(Sketch by Roy Kerridge)

The Spiritual Baptist Church

Encouraged by this, the bespectacled young man took advantage of a halt in the singing and began to Testify in a booming voice.

"My parents brought me to London from Trinidad when I was a child, and they taught me to love Jesus! Jesus is my all-in-all! He is Shango, for only my God can make the thunder! Jesus is the Lord! He is Shango! He is God!"

"Amen" those around him repeated dutifully, then turned to a tall woman, Mother Persecutor herself, who sang a slow, high-pitched eerie song.

> "I weep! I moan!
> I don't want to walk it alone!
> I'm just a mourning pilgrim
> Trying to reach my Heavenly home!"

No one had seemed surprised to hear Jesus compared to Shango, the Yoruba god of thunder. In Trinidad, this deity is worshipped openly and perhaps equated with Jesus. Shango churches have not as yet appeared in Britain, as far as I know. Spiritual Baptists seem to form a Trinidadian half-way mark between out-and-out African Shangoism and everyday Caribbean Pentecostalism. All the same, I had never heard Jesus compared with Shango before, although a Jamaican had once told me "Jesus is my obeah-man" (witchdoctor).

A shadow fell across the doorway, that of the first coach. Bishop Powell hurried outside, spoke to the two drivers, a Sikh and a Cockney, and then prepared for the mass embarkation and Exodus. Ringing his handbell imperiously, he led the blindfolded Candidates and their Nurses to the front coach, followed by robed Mothers and visiting pastors. There was a religious coach for the church hierarchy and a secular coach for mere holiday visitors to Eastbourne.

I took care to squeeze into the holy coach, amid flapping tent-like white robes, where I breathed in the smell of hot candle grease and incense. A black-clad pastor sat next to me, and asked me if I had an aspirin.

"I've been on an all-night vigil for the Candidates, and it's given me a headache", he explained, clutching at the scarlet headband on his brow.

Luckily, I had a Paracetamol tablet left over from breakfast, and it seemed to effect a cure. For as we bowled along through the gracious streets of early morning London, he joined in the Mount Pisgah Coach Travelling Song.

> "Go before us, Lord, go before us,
> And do Thy will Thyself!
> Roll Jordan, Roll!
> Roll, Jor-dan, Roll!
> I want to go to Heaven when I die
> Just to hear sweet Jordan roll!"

The poor unfortunate day-trippers in the following coach had no perpetual sing-song, nor did they dance in the aisle. Everybody who could do so had squeezed into the holy coach.

Unfortunately, not far from Eastbourne, the driver took a wrong turning, and mild panic ensued. Soon he found a signpost marked "Eastbourne", and spirits rallied. All this while, Brother Ricky beat his drum and led out with strange Trinidadian choruses.

> "You can talk about this, you can talk about that,
> But you can't go to Heaven as you like! (Not at all!)
> For the angels in Heaven have a record,
> And you can't go to Heaven as you like."

Majestic downland scenery aroused no interest in the Mount Pisgah-ites. The South Downs dominated the horizon, a barrier between us and the sea. Whenever I pointed out items of interest in the surrounding farmland, the pastor and others thought I was only wondering if we were going in the right direction. In this way, a llama in a field, a windmill by the roadside and the Long Man of Wilmington, a prehistoric giant etched from a chalk hill, all passed unnoticed. At last we reached the suburbs of Eastbourne, and then the seafront itself. Slowly we moved along past flowerbeds, hotels and holidaymakers, as the driver looked out for the stopping-point. Still Brother Ricky drummed and sang.

> "Have you a passport to Heaven gate?
> Have you a passport to Heaven gate?
> If you haven't got one, you ought to get one,
> Have you a passport to Heaven gate?"

We stopped at last, beside a hut marked "Lifeboat Exhibition", near a sloping lawn where a stage had been erected for a children's show. A lot was going on that day, and our strip of beach, with bathing huts at prom level, had been taped off to prevent the Sea Baptism colliding with a lifeboat demonstration. Bishop Powell and his bell led the Candidates to the shore, pausing only to allow a Toytown train-load of child passengers to rattle by. Cobbles led down to our bit of beach, and the Sea Baptism began, with a church service held around the transported Mount Pisgah altar table, set down on the shingle.

Purposefully, Bishop Powell picked up three stones from the beach and faced the placid breakers. The tide was about to come in. Taking care to miss paddling children, he threw the stones in one by one. Church members called out, "One for the Father! One for the Son! And one for the Holy Ghost!"

Only now was the ocean safe for himself and three assistants to enter – two pastors in black, and Mother Jewel in scarlet robes and a red, blue and yellow turban. Two staffs and two crosses, each one man-high, were carried far into the sea and then planted to stake out the baptising territory. Mother Jewel struggled bravely to set her staff upright, waves breaking over her shoulders. Despite having a steel point, designed for piercing the sea bed, the staff kept falling down and floating away. At one point, Mother Jewel was nearly carried out to sea, clinging to the holy staff as a shipwrecked sailor clings to an oar. No wonder the crowds of holidaymakers ignored the dinghies and overhead helicopters of the lifesavers, so close by, and stared with amazement at the doings of Mount Pisgah.

Meanwhile, at the altar table, the service went on. People from the secular coach gathered with hymn books in a semi-circle around the robed holy ones at the altar. The blindfolded Candidates, all in a row holding lit candles, could not see to read the hymns, but hummed and swayed as best as they could. Bishop Powell and the pastors returned, dripping wet but confident. Now the baptism could begin!

Head erect, feet stumbling, the first candidate, a young girl, was led to the sea by her personal Nurse. Of what was she thinking, beneath her blindfold? As she waded in, the Bishop before her, the whole church began to sing, a mournful wailing cry.

> "Jordan River
> Chilly and cold!
> Chills the body
> But not the soul!
> And every time I feel the Spirit
> Moving in my heart I want to pray."

Watched by the two pastors, Bishop Powell seized the girl and swooshed her backwards under the water, not once but three times. The third time, he held her under so long that I imagined I could see bubbles. She was not the only one to hold her breath, for some of the church members on the beach looked distinctly worried. But up she came, a pastor removed her blindfold and she greeted the world with a cry of "Glory!" Then she was helped, staggering, to a changing hut to put on dry clothes, as a new joyous song was sung by all.

> "He arose! He arose!
> With a cry of triumph o'er His foes!
> He arose the victor o'er the dark domain,
> And He lives forever with the saints to reign.
> He arose! He arose!
> Hallelujah, Christ arose!"

The same two songs, "Jordan River" and "He Arose" were sung for the entering and emerging of each Candidate. Brother Cedric took the plunge without mishap. Afro-hair, still jogging and dancing, was accorded the great honour of being swung up in the air and hurled down on his back with a splash, when his turn came. He could hardly walk when the Bishop and pastors had finished with him, but willing hands half-carried him to the hut. A heavy woman Candidate needed not one but five Nurses to steady her back up the steep shingle to her hut.

Bishop Powell and the pastors waited in the sea for the Candidates to be brought to them. Now and then, the Bishop rang his handbell. Once he nearly lost it on the seabed, which would have been a calamity, since it was needed afterwards as a chalice, when the Candidates drank seawater. So holy was the sea, now he had prayed over it, that the Bishop splashed water over the Candidates' heads as they came up for air. The last three women showed clean pairs of heels, for he up-ended them like dabbling ducks, their bare feet the last to disappear beneath the waves. And all the while, the mournful chant rang out:

> "Jordan Ri-ver,
> Chilly and cold!"

Holidaymakers, utterly fascinated, crowded against the strip of tape that, together with a roughly chalked board of wood, proclaimed the segment of beach to be "Reserved for Mount Pisgah Baptism". The council had provided this sign, a source of great pride to the church. "We are happy to be recognised by the people of Eastbourne – they give us our own sign!" Mother Jewel proclaimed. "We greet the good people of Eastbourne! You may wonder why it is a fine day, when the radio predicted rain, but it is thanks to our prayers and a merciful God!"

Some of those who pressed around were West Indian holidaymakers, members of a different church.

"We are Moravians", one of them, an elderly man, told a Mother Shepherdess of Mount Pisgah. "In the Moravian Church we do things a bit different. Why do you carry staffs, and what does the writing on them mean?"

"Greetings, Moravian Brethren! We carry rod and staff because the Psalmist say 'My rod and staff they comfort thee'. The 'seals' or secret writing is holy, and is for when the staff is laid on a sick person for healing." These explanations satisfied the friendly Moravians, whose sect, I believe, originated in Germany.

> "Chills the bod-ee
> But not the sou-oul".

Now "Jordan River" was sung for the last time, and the new life jubilation of "He Arose" signalled the end of the baptism. Bishop, pastors and Mother Jewel held hands in a circle in deep water – then all plunged forwards head first, to emerge floating face downward as if a circle of petals, still holding hands. Then, tired but happy, they made for the changing-huts. Church people sought out deck chairs and ice cream vendors, and a more relaxed atmosphere prevailed. The lifeboatsmen had long retired, discouraged by a disc jockey on the nearby stage playing a Jamaican tune, "Brown Girl in the Ring", followed by the carnival soca song from Trinidad "Hot, Hot, Hot". English children formed a conga line and danced across the green.

While parts of Eastbourne had been taken over by the Caribbean, the sea and the sandy foreshore seemed resolutely and nineteen thirtyishly English. Blond mop-haired children paddled, built sand castles and dug deep moats around them. It was delightful to see the pleasure they took from natural things, sun, sea, sand and sky, helped along by plastic buckets and spades. Mount Pisgah children, perhaps inspired by their Leader, threw pebbles into the sea.

A mother Shepherdess took Brother Ricky to task over his 'T' shirt, "I'm a Forking Trinidadian".

"It says 'forking', 'cos the devil in the picture carry a fork, innit?" he said, aggrieved.

"But Brother Ricky, why carry a picture of Satan on you?"

"Ha! It may be a devil, but it's not Satan!"

"Brother Ricky, Brother Ricky, why you call yourself a Trinidadian when you come from Grenada?"

"I spent years in Trinidad, that's me home! Man, the Spiritual Baptist churches there are out of this world!"

All the same, the flamboyant drummer was persuaded by his wife to put on a jacket. Disgruntled, he lit a cigarette and was at once dragged by his young wife to a faraway bench where the Mothers couldn't see him.

I went to look at the changed - and - dry Candidates, who all sat in deck chairs, the women dressed in white gowns with lace and veils. Most seemed contented, despite having had to drink sea water from a bell and a gourd. None of them spoke, or acknowledged my presence, but later one of them told me that they had promised to be totally silent until the Final Prayer.

For this prayer, the Bishop lined all the Candidates in a row, and then appealed to the crowd of sightseers leaning over the railings, "Don't the Sisters look like brides?"

Indeed they did, the relit candles burning with orange daylight flames against the billowing white of their robes. The tide advanced swiftly, and the altar table had to be carried uphill for a few yards before the farewell service could take place.

Coach drivers honked, the ocean claimed the beach, and I helped little Granny Wilkins up the steps into the coach for a musical journey back to London. Back at Mount Pisgah Church at last, the entrance hung mysteriously with leaves and boughs, the Brethren prepared for more hours of worship. But I prepared for home and bed. It had been a full day, and my dreams were filled with sweet church choruses, with golden pens, Heaven gates and Jordan rivers.

Sounds of singing, dancing and prayer could be heard whenever I passed Mount Pisgah with my dog at night. A week after the baptisms, when things seemed to have quietened down, I looked into the little church once more. The service was over, and a few members sat around talking, while children played. Bishop Powell, engrossed in conversation with Mother Persecutor, wore black robes, a bell hanging from his neck. I recognised one of the baptised candidates, Sister June.

"It was a wonderful day - I feel so full of glory", she confided. "All the discipline and rehearsing was well worth while".

"She call herself a Shepherdess! Ha!" I could hear Mother Persecutor saying. Diffidently, thirteen year old Shadrach, a well-dressed slim boy with an air of humorous reserve, approached me.

"It's about my Dad", he said. "He tells me and my sister funny stories when we're in bed at night, and he wondered if you could get them put in a book".

"You mean like the Uncle Remus stories?" I said, but no one at Mount Pisgah had heard of Uncle Remus.

Shadrach's father, Deacon Tony Henry was an important member of the church. A tall strong man, in black robes and a vivid red headband, he had never impressed me very much. He approached every task with a deliberate, serious air that I had mistaken for surliness. But now, I found, Deacon Tony had hidden depths. As he spoke, his supposedly impassive features warmed into friendliness, his tongue unleashed, betrayed its owner as a master conversationalist.

"Back home in Jamaica, the moon is not like the moon here in England", he began. "It bright, so bright that back in the 'fifties people would walk anywhere at night. Sunday evening, the people would walk back from church along the middle o' the road, singing and talking, with someone playing a banjo."

"The moon did make everything silver, you know, almost light like day. So when me was about Shadrach age, twelve and thirteen, I'd meet my friends and us boys would sit in the middle of the road, in the night time, and tell stories. So I'll tell you these stories now, and you can put them in a book for me."

"Once on a time, there was a young couple, very much in love, and engaged to be married. Such a beautiful girl, and such a tall good-looking young man!

"Now the girl had a garden with a summer house, and one day she went in the summer house and lay down on a couch there. She looked up and saw a big beam of wood stretching right across the ceiling, holding it up, you know.

"So she said to herself, 'Oh my, just look at that big beam of wood on the ceiling! Supposing me and my dear young man got married and he came in here and lay down on this couch! That big beam of wood might break, might fall down, baddam! and kill my dear sweet husband! If he was dead, whatever would I do?"

She began to cry and cry. By and by, along came she boyfriend, he hears her crying and run inside.

'What's the matter?'

'Oh, oh, oh!' she cry. 'I was just thinking, my dear, that if we were married and you came in here and lay on this couch, that big beam o' wood might fall on your head, baddam! and kill you! Then whatever would I do? Oh, oh, oh!' and she cry worse than ever.

'Stupid woman!' said the young man. He was disgusted, he thought she was so stupid.

'You are so stupid that I'm going to pack my bag and roam the whole world, and never come back to marry you at all unless I meet a woman who is more stupid than what you is'.

So he pack his bag and leave, travelling, travelling. Before long, he met an old woman who lived far off on she own, in a wooden house, and have a cow. So when the man meet her, she trying to push the cow up on a ladder onto the roof of the house! A cow up a ladder, can you imagine?

'Young man, help me get me cow up me ladder onto me roof', she beg. 'Look, the roof is covered with green grass growing up there on it, but me cow can't reach. So help me get the cow up'.

The young man was surprised! He began to laugh.

'Is why you don't pick the grass and bring it down?' he ask her.

'Oh, I never thought of that!'

To himself the young man say 'This is a stupid woman!' She is more stupid than me girlfriend is'.

So he ran home, he told his girlfriend 'sorry' and they get married and live happily with never a cross word. Ha, I wish I could o' seen that old woman pushing a cow up a ladder! I'd have laughed and laughed!"

I tried to remember a story my Jamaican friend Mrs. Brown had once told me, about two sailors who got on a church roof and played on trumpets just as the preacher was warning the people about Judgement Day.

"They stamped the church," I concluded.

"Ha, very good, but do you know *this* one! Does you ever hear about a character name Brother Anancy, half a man and half a spider, greedy and bad?"

"I think I am acquainted with that notable personality", I replied.

"In the place where Anancy live, one time, food was very, very scarce. Anancy left his children at home, hungry, and decided to look for food. He search and search, and finally he finds a whole heap o'yams growing in a secret place in the bush. So he cook and eat. Next day he do the same. But then he begins to think about his hungry children at home.

'Maybe I had better share the yam with me pickney', he decide.

"So next night, he bring the yam home, and clean them and cook them there. All the children mouth water, you know! Finally Anancy speak.

'Now children, whoever can tell me the name o' the yam can eat the yam'

"They all guessed one name and another, but no one could guess.

'I'm sorry,' say Anancy, and ate up all the yam.

"Next evening, it was the same story: 'Tell me the name o' the yam and you can eat', but nobody can do it. Days went by, and Anancy got fat and sleek, and the children skin and bone.

"Finally one clever boy follow Anancy, hiding behind trees, until he find Anancy's yam-place. When Anancy had picked some yam and gone, the boy get some okra pod an' smear it on a flat stone near the yams. It slippy, you know! He covered the flat stone with leaves. Next day, he follow Anancy again.

"Anancy pick an armful o' yam, but then he step on the flat slippery stone, he slip, he fall over and cry out 'Oh Lord, me fall an' mash up me Sesame Yam!'

"So when the little boy hear this, he run for home, an' get there before Anancy. In come Anancy, he cook the yam and say, 'Now if any o' you pickney know the name o' the yam, you can have it.'

"All the pickney cry 'Sesame Yam!' in one loud shout, they take all o' the yam and eat, eat, eat!"

"That's a good story", I said. "My friend Mrs. Brown once told me that when there was a famine in Brother Anancy's country, the Anancy family only had three bananas, one for each o' the three children and none for Anancy. Anancy looked so hungry, that the children said 'Let's give him half of our food.' So each child gave Anancy half a banana. But instead of having half the food, Anancy had more, 'cos he had one and a half bananas, and the children had only half a banana each."

"Anancy wins again!" said the Deacon, with relish. "This talk of children reminds me, there was a mother who had three children, Big Head, Big Belly and Fine Foot."

Annabelle, Shadrach's seven year old sister, had somehow become a wide-eyed part of our audience.

"Fine Foot", she repeated softly to herself, in quiet appreciation.

"They were funny-looking children", the Deacon continued, ruminatively. "Big Head had a too-big head, Big Belly (who was a girl) had a giant round belly, an' Fine Foot was nearly all feet, you know. So the mother took them to the doctor and he said, 'Don't let these children get excited! 'Cos if they get excited, and move fast, then Big Head will break his head, Big Belly will burst her belly and Fine Foot will split to pieces.' So the mother warned the children.

"But the very next day they went out walking, and Big Head saw a mango tree loaded with fruit. He looked up at the mango, and bim! his neck cracked and his head fell an' hung upside-down his back!

"When Big Belly saw this, she laughed so much she burst! So Fine Foot run home to tell his mother!"

Here the Deacon paused, and looked at me triumphantly, before delivering the punch-line.

"That was the end of the whole family!" he cried, shaking with merriment.

Annabelle laughed, hopped and hugged herself in glee, even though she had heard the story before. I found myself unable to cap this terrible story, and so I feared that the session must draw to a close. Later, I remembered a story told to me by a Ghanaian friend, that rivalled the Deacon's abrupt family saga in its sheer finality.

A mother had told a big boy to look after her small child, leaving him a bird to roast for the infant's dinner. But the big boy was absent minded, so he roasted the little boy by mistake, and tried to feed him to the bird. The bird wouldn't eat such food, so in a rage, the ill-chosen babysitter roasted and ate the bird as a punishment. What the mother said when she came home has not been recorded. I'm not quite sure that I understand the Ghanaian sense of humour.

Needing no prompting, however, the Deacon at once launched into another story. He was in a great good humour, and so was I. This was my kind of Deacon!

"One time, Brother Anancy and Brother Takuma sat down to share a big tub of butter."

"Who was Brother Takuma?" I asked.

"I don't know. Maybe he was a frog. Anyway, they sat down to share the butter. Anancy say 'You lick round the edges and I'll dip in the middle.'

"Takuma thought that this seemed fair, so he sat down and began to lick. Then he sees that while he just licks, Anancy is scooping up big handfuls from the middle and eating up all the butter. So Takuma suddenly put out he hand and take a big dip from the middle! Anancy jump up in a rage, and give him a great lick round the head, BADDAM! Takuma fall over like he dead, an' just lie there.

"Now Anancy begin to catch 'fraid. He say, 'Wake up, Brother Takuma, me didn't mean to hit you so hard." Takuma lie there. Anancy try an' revive Takuma but he can't do it. So he runs away. When Anancy gone, Takuma sat up, quite recovered, and ate up all the butter!

After that, he walk slowly after Anancy, like he dead and stumblin', staring forward, arms out like this. (Deacon Tony posed as a sleepwalking zombie). He chase Anancy, wailing, 'You no hear the news? Anancy kill Takuma! You no hear the news? Anancy kill Takuma!

So the table was turned on Brother Anancy that time!"

A turbaned Mother began to shoo us out, for the church was closing. In the doorway, Annabelle looked up at a new sign on the wall that read 'Spiritual Healing Centre.'

"Everyone going to get healed!" she cried, and gave a little skipping dance.

"More stories after church tomorrow night", her father promised us all.

On the way home, I remembered that Brother Takuma wasn't a frog at all. In Ghana, the original home of Anancy stories, Takuma is Anancy's son. But this fact has been forgotten somewhere along the passage to Jamaica.

Deacon Tony Henry was as good as his word. While church Mothers cleared away chairs in the background, the Deacon settled down to tell the story of Anancy at Bird Cherry Island. Annabelle and I hung on his every word, but Shadrach felt himself to be a bit too grown-up for such proceedings. He looked benign but condescending, and sat a little way away, occasionally pretending that he wasn't listening. The Deacon kept stopping to laugh and slap his knees at various parts of his story, but somehow the tale was told.

"Anancy lived near a big lake, and in the middle of the lake was an island called Bird Cherry Island. Every day, a big flock of blackbird would fly over to the island to eat the cherries that grow on the trees there. Anancy was friend with the blackbird, and he wanted to go to Bird Cherry Island with them and eat cherries. So he asked if they would take him.

"If we each give you a feather, you can fly with us', say the blackbird dem. 'But you must be ready to fly back with us when we go home again, for we won't wait.'

'No problem!' say Anancy.

"So each o' the many, many blackbird pull out a feather an' stick it in Anancy. When he is covered in black feather, he find he can fly! So he fly with them to Bird Cherry Island and gorge and gorge himself on cherry until he fall asleep on the limb o' the cherry tree.

"At sunset, the blackbird get together for the flight back. But Anancy won't wake up. They poke and they peck, but he just snores. So then each blackbird take his feather, put it back on, and fly away. When Anancy wake up, he is all alone, and no feather to fly with; stuck on the island!

"He goes to the water, look at it, then take a leaf an' drop it in. 'If the leaf can float, so can I', he say.

"The leaf float, so Anancy jump on it, but then it sink! He go down, down, down, until he reach the bottom of the lake. Then he start to walk, and after a while, he see a light. He follow the light and so he come to Alligator Town. Inside the Alligator Town, it quite dry an' nice.

"He knock at the door of Brother Alligator house, and when the Alligator come out, Anancy say, as bold as brass, 'Hallo, friend Alligator, I is your cousin, come to visit with you.'

"Alligator greet him, but say 'Hmm, if you is really my cousin, you can eat scalding hot porridge straight from the pot, just like I do. Let me have a test now, to see if you are my true cousin.'

"So the Alligator get two pot o' scalding hot porridge, one for himself, one for Anancy. He tip the pot up, ate his scalding porridge, licked his lips, then pushed the other scalding pot to Anancy. There was steam pouring off it, you know!

'Brother Alligator, what are you playing at? This is cold porridge for a man like me', say Anancy. 'Put it outside in the sun and it will get hotter.'

"So the Alligator put the pot outside, and after a while, brought it in for Anancy. Of course, outside the pot had grown cool, not hot.

'It still too cold!" complained Anancy, after he had taste the porridge and burnt his tongue. 'Put it outside in the sun once more.'

"After a time, Brother Alligator brought the porridge indoors, where Anancy grabbed and ate it.

'Ah, that's hot enough!' he said, but it was really cold.

'Now I see you are truly my cousin', Alligator cried. 'But the only room where you can stay is with my six eggs. Would you mind washing them for me, every day?'

"Of course, Anancy agree. No sooner is he alone with the six crocodile eggs than he cook and eat five of them, just leaving one. Next day Brother Alligator say, 'Let me see my six egg', so Anancy say, 'Just wait, I'm washing them one at a time.'

"Anancy wash the one egg, go outside and say 'Look, Cousin Alligator, here's the first one.'

"Then he take the egg in his room, dirty it and wash it again, then say, 'Look, Cousin Alligator, here is the second egg.' So he fool the poor Alligator by showing him the same egg six times. Every day he go through the same thing, pretending to wash six eggs one at a time, but in reality he wash one egg six times. Brother Alligator suspects nothing.

"After a time, Anancy persuade the Alligator to let him go home. Brother Alligator has two big sons, but one is deaf and the other is hard of hearing. The Alligator tell the two sons to row Anancy back to his side of the lake, in a boat. Just before leaving, Anancy slip away and eat the last egg!

"Off they go, the two sons rowing and Anancy sitting in the boat, when the old Alligator discover all his eggs are missing! At once he roars to his sons, 'Bring back Anancy!'

"Anancy hear him plain and loud, but the two sons can't hear properly, since one is deaf and the other is hard of hearing.

'What is our father saying?' them ask Anancy.

'He's saying 'Storm ahead! Go faster! There's a big storm coming! Go faster!'

"So the brothers row faster. Again, the father roar out 'Bring back Anancy!' Again, the brothers ask Anancy what he say, and Anancy reply 'Go faster! Storm ahead! Storm ahead!'

(At this point, Deacon Henry shook with laughter, repeating 'Storm ahead' to himself, and laughing again, his eyes shining with mirth).

"Soon they safely reach, and Anancy step ashore on dry land. He invite the brothers to join him.

'Let me have a trial of strength', he tell them. 'Look, I'll get into this bag and you whirl me round and round and see if I get giddy.'

The two Alligator sons agree, so Anancy take a big bag and climb inside. They whirl him round and round, and finally stop. Anancy climb out and pretend he's not giddy by holding on a tree with one hand.

'See, I'm not giddy! I'm a man!' he say. 'Now you try.'

"So the two Alligator sons climb into the same bag together. Anancy take the bag and whirl it round and round, then dash it against a tree!"

Here Deacon Henry stopped, in a dramatic pause, and looked at us triumphantly.

"Did he kill them?" I blurted out anxiously, breaking the awe-struck silence.

"And cook them! And' eat them! That Anancy! Oh my! No wonder they calls him Anancy the Trickster! Yes, they calls him the Trickster!"

Story time was over, for the church had soon to be locked up. Deacon Henry's accent became more English, as he fell out of the storytelling trance. Such an exciting story warranted a breathless present-tense approach.

As I was wishing everyone goodnight, two boys of eleven or twelve rode by on BMX bikes, and stopped outside the door. One of the Church Mothers took them to task for being out so late. It was almost midnight. With her Mother Hubbard clothes, the church lady seemed to be separated from the two trainer-and-cap schoolboys not by a generation but by centuries.

"You should be at home studying!" she cried.

"It's too hot to stay indoors", one of the boys mumbled.

"Ha! In four years time you could be solicitors! What do you want to do when you leave school?"

"Sell drugs", the taller of the two boys replied, with bravado. The two rode off laughing. The Mother glanced indignantly at the boys and then at Deacon Henry, as if hoping that the latter could conjure up Anancy to put the boys in a sack.

Several months later, in the wintertime, I heard of the sad death of Bishop Powell of Mount Pisgah Spiritual Baptist Church. My informant was the Bishop's friend, the impressive and portentous Evangelist Wiltshire, who presides over prayer meetings in her gloomy East End flat. Dressed in robes and turban, she speaks and preaches in a slow, awe-inspiring and lugubrious manner.

Over tea, rice and corned beef, the Evangelist announced her plans of collecting money for homeless young people. She had seen a television programme in which the plight of young drug addicts and helpless youngsters turned out of Children's Homes had been blamed on the government's housing policy.

"Me so sorry when I see the young people dem, in cardboard boxes, on television. Them have no place at all to live, and it's all because of Huss."

"Huss?" I queried. It sounded like a kind of fish. Or was that a hake?

"Huss black people!" she explained. "Huss black people have come over and taken all the council flat! White people have nowhere to go".

Quickly I changed the subject, before she could quote Enoch Powell about the Tizer foaming with much fizz, or whatever it was. Like many churchy Jamaicans of an older generation, she was absurdly pro-white, and very censorious of other West Indians.

"Have you heard from Bishop Powell lately?" I asked.

"What, you no hear that he die? Yes, he die some weeks ago now, after a trip round the West Indies ordaining ministers and robing Mothers. Poor Bishop Powell is no more here on earth. For years, many people trying to put something on him, but he was always too clever. I wonder why he slip up now, an' get obeahed at last. Them call it 'cancer', but I know the Bishop had his enemies, and it is obeah (witchcraft) that have finished the poor man."

Overcome with sympathy for her friend the Bishop, Evangelist Wiltshire removed her bottom teeth and waved them in the air as if to make her point more clear.

"Yes, they have got the poor Bishop at last. You and I must go to the funeral next week Friday. Mother Jewel, his wife, have got the Bishop right there in Mount Pisgah church, lying in state. But me and Mother Jewel don't see heye to heye (eye to eye), as she is jealous o'me, you know. Bishop Powell always have a nice word for me."

"I'll go along and pay my respects tomorrow night", I told the Evangelist.

That was on a Monday, so next evening I walked down the road to Mount Pisgah, reflecting on the flamboyant noisy jollity of Bishop Powell, a jollity I would know no more. I did not yet realise that it had now been replaced by the flamboyant noisy jollity of the bereaved widow, Mother Jewel, a jollity with a sharper edge to it.

At the door of Mount Pisgah, I ducked my head under two shepherd's crooks fixed in the doorway, their hooks crossing, forming an arch. Laurel leaves hung from the hooks like mistletoe. Once inside, blinking back at the many candles, I found a seat and sat surrounded by white-robed mourners. Suddenly I became aware of the coffin, raised on a table between the centre pole and the altar. The lid was closed, and decorated like a banquetting table, with a white lace cloth, candles and silverware. Three pairs of shepherd's crooks with linked hooks stood upright by its side. "In Sympathy" cards stood among the candlesticks on the lid.

Mother Jewel's face shone red beneath her turban; she seemed filled with fierce energy, greeting everybody and announcing songs, prayers and readings in a vivacious "end of the pier" manner.

"Precious Memories!" she barked, and the church sang softly.

"Precious Memories - how they linger..."

"Yes, we have Precious Memories of our dear Bishop!" she exclaimed, when the song was over. "Have patience, children, you will all see him. Every day up to the burial on Friday, I open him up at noon for two hours, and at six o'clock in the evening for two hours. Yes, I wake him up in the morning for breakfast, and at night I wake him again. But I put him to bed at eight, so come early. People will come to stare, I know, and not all come with a sorrowful heart. Enemies will think that now little Mount Pisgah is weak, but we must take no notice. All the same, mothers, don't let your children accept or eat food offered by a stranger. You all know why, I shall say no more. Another chorus, please - Lonesome Valley!"

"You've got to walk that Lonesome Valley, you've got to walk it for yourself', sang the mourners.

Swaying slowly to the rhythm, most of the church members and visitors arose and joined hands around the coffin. A young girl, dressed in a pure white nun's habit, announced in a tragic voice that an angel had appeared to her in a dream.

"The angel tell me the Bishop must be bury in his shepherd robe!"

"True revelation!" someone cried.

"Fear not, he will be buried in such a fashion!" Mother Jewel called out, to groans of assent.

"Jordan River, chilly and cold" arose as a chilling farewell song in a hundred throats. Hands unlinked, and the mourners swayed, each caught up in a solo dance.
"I too have a vision!" Mother Jewel shouted. "On the burial day, let no children play or run around in the cemetery. There is a hole! They will fall in the water! Mount Pisgah sing 'The First Trumpet Sounds'!"

Somewhere out of sight, bongo drums pattered, then rolled out a steady rhythm.

> "Where shall I be when the First Trumpet Sounds?
> Where shall I be when it sounds so loud?"

Deacon Henry, Anancy forgotten, began to dance quickly, back bent, knees and elbows swinging. A Mother Shepherdess in blue and white robes danced as if she were digging a grave there and then, seeming to mime the actions of a spade.

> "It sounds so loud, it can raise the very dead,
> Oh, where shall I be when it sounds?"

After a time, the rhythm stepped up, augmented by tambourines. A Rasta visitor, with a chirpy but unchurchy girlfriend, seemed to be thoroughly enjoying himself.

In high delight, Mother Jewel shouted, "Now you're in school! Now you're getting wise! You are learning from Ezekiel, that one-foot prophet! You see Bishop Powell lying over there? His spirit has gone into me! I am Unisex now!"

When the dance slowed down, Sister Jackie, a great friend of Bishop Powell, stepped forward and began to testify, or deliver a message handed to her by God.
"Do you remember, church, how Bishop Powell lay while he was dying, with all us gathered round? He nearly slipped away, but we encouraged him, and he came back and tarried a short while. And when he tarried, he rebuked us, looking up and smiling.

'The chariots!' he cry. 'The angels! They were coming for me! Why didn't you let me go?'

"You see, the angels came, but our praying made them go. We should sing 'Sweet Chariot', the song our Bishop loved..."

Swiftly, Mother Jewel picked up a pair of bongo drums, held them on high and announced, " 'Sweet Chariot' is our farewell song for Bishop Powell!"

Everybody in the church began to sing the slow, sweet spiritual. It was the first time I had heard "Swing Low" in its natural setting, so to speak, so I looked and listened with interest. I wondered if Bishop Powell's spirit, hovering near, could hear and enjoy the song. Nobody else, I am sure, had any doubts on the subject whatsoever – except perhaps some of the merry, sceptical children.

> "Swing Low, Sweet Chario-o-ot,
> Coming for to carry me home,
> Swing Low, Sweet Chario-o-ot,
> Coming for to carry me home."

Instantly the church began to dance, as if hypnotised. Even I swayed slightly. A moment later, the Holy Spirit arrived, but among those who jerked, groaned or spoke in tongues, there remained several people able to sing "Swing Low" over and over again. One of the women, a wiry little old lady, in shawl, apron and headscarf, allowed the Spirit to ride her like a horse. Down on her hands and knees she dropped, and in a fog of Holy Ghost tragedy, she noisily bumped her way round and round the centre pole on all fours, singing loudly all the while.

> "I looked up over yonder, and what did I see?
> Coming for to carry me home,
> A band of angels coming after me!
> Coming for to carry me home."

Wednesday
A surprise was in store for me when I reached the door of Mount Pisgah, for there stood a huge bearded bishop in full regalia, ringing a handbell.

"Mourn, Israel!" he commanded, in a voice very like that of the late Bishop Powell. I stood transfixed, almost thinking I saw a ghost, and one of the Mothers sidled up to me.
"That is Bishop Powell's first cousin, just flown in from Grenada", she whispered. "He is a

Bishop over there, in the Spiritual Baptist Church - Bishop Jacob Powell."

The deceased was named Bishop Victor Emmanuel Powell. Awe-stricken, I faltered before Bishop Jacob's ferocious gaze. He looked rather like an Aborigine elder or Papuan village chief, a mighty man with a large bushy beard, eyebrows and moustache, unevenly grizzled in ashy-grey patches. As the Mother and I entered, his stern features softened while he greeted us, bending his head slightly as if doffing his great chesspiece-bishop's hat.

Mother Jewel now appeared demure and self-effacing, as the new Bishop took command, roaring out orders for brethren to "come right up yere and read from the Bible!"
"Let the coffin be open!" he announced next, ringing his bell.

The lid was at once cleared of ornaments and raised. Everyone crowded forward, with me the last, and I saw the late Bishop lying on a crimson cloth, dressed in crimson robes, dwindled in body but kingly in black-bearded repose, his eyes closed. Members rushed forward to wave church flags over the body. Some flags were yellow, others checkered in black and white, like racing car flags. Both men and women leaned over and kissed the corpse's cheeks. Nothing could disturb the Bishop's air of calm, but even so, the new Bishop roared out words of restraint.

"I shall raise a chorus!" he boomed. "Where am I bound for?"

"Bound for Jerusalem!" the church chanted in response.

Bishop Jacob: "I'm Bound for Jerusalem! Passing through Africa! Where am I bound for?"

Church: "Bound for Jerusalem!"

Bishop Jacob: "I'm Bound for Jerusalem! Passing through India! Where am I bound for?"

Church: "Bound for Jerusalem."

Bishop Jacob: "I'm Bound for Jerusalem! Passing through China!"

Once more, the whole church began to dance, a foot-shuffling flag-waving ring shout, around the coffin and the centre pole. Finally the song petered out in errant wails, and we took our seats once more. Bishop Jacob stood before us, holding a shepherd's crook and looking fiercely majestic, like a Russian bishop about to anoint a Tsar. Appearances were not deceptive, for he announced the ordination of the new Pastor and Leader who would take his departed cousin's place as overlord of Mount Pisgah.

"Step forward, Deacon Tony Henry! Kneel!"

I gaped, as my good friend the story-telling Deacon came forward to accept his honours and new responsibility. Brother Anancy seemed a long way away.

Taking a wet candlestick from a vase of flowers, the ordaining Bishop bent over and made sacred markings on the carpeted floor, in wax. Among the many symbols, I could see a pyramid with a many-branched tree on either side, and a cross before it.

"Signed, sealed and delivered", whispered the Mother who had met me at the door.

Pressing the bell on the new Leader's head, the cousin-Bishop anointed olive-oil around it, then anointed those who kneeled around. Sister Jackie read the passage aloud from the Bible, where Samuel finds Saul and anoints him King. After reading one line, Sister Jackie paused, and the cousin-Bishop repeated the same line in a hoarse musical roar. Perhaps this dual form of Bible-reading, like "lining out" songs originated in the days when only one or two church members knew how to read. Whatever the case, it seemed to recast the Bible passages as a chant-and-response work song.

Leader Henry, as he now was, continued to kneel before the centre pole, and was to remain there for over an hour. A lit candle was placed on top of his head, which must have been uncomfortable. Whenever it went out, a solicitous Mother stepped forward and relit it. Luckily, the candle was wreathed in flowers and perched on top of a golden ball, or Iota, that symbolised the world, and these adornments must have absorbed some of the hot wax. The Leader himself had to hold the candle and trimmings in place while kneeling. I felt sorry for the poor man, whose high office was earned by cramps and suffering.

Annabelle, his little daughter, looked on wide-eyed. Obviously the sight of her father's strange ordeal was making a deep impression on her. In one hand, she clutched a tambourine, the canvas inscribed in large letters: "This Tambourine belongs to Annabelle, a gift from Granny Wilkins, and no one is allowed to touch it At All." Little Granny Wilkins sat nearby, red-eyed, weeping for her son-in-law in his open coffin.

Concluding the Bible reading, the bearded Bishop approached the candle-lit man and pronounced words of wisdom in a solemn, awe-inspiring tone.

"My brother, always be humble. There is no true picture of Jesus, for there was no camera in His day. No one knows what He look like, but you must keep Him in mind. Help the Rasta, the dope addict, the mugger and the thief."

At these words, a visiting Rasta lowered his eyes modestly, as if deeply honoured.
"Do not be proud", the Bishop continued. "Respect ordinary people and remember the Sermon on the Mount."

Suddenly he seemed to remember the song "Steal Away to Jesus", and sang a line or two, then preached, then sang, and finally compromised by speaking in a sing-song voice. Every time he paused at the end of a chant, members of the congregation would loudly intone "My God!" in the same sing-song voice, full of mystery and sincerity.

"The trumpet sound within my soul! I don't have long to stay here! Steal away - my brethren, there was a time I cared nothing for the Lord! I only liked to have a good time. Then one day, in a dancehall, I came to myself, I looked around and all the other people seemed strange. I felt sorry for them. I thought 'Why am I here?' The very next day, I go to church and ask to be baptise. ("My God!") Yes, brethren, I was Baptise, but after a while, I go on back to the same dancehall. You see, I broke my promise to the Lord and I became ill. When I was better, I returned to church, this time never to leave! I never get weary yet! My dear cousin, Bishop Powell, he took the same road as I, but he has gone further on down the road."

With that, he sang anew, as bongo drums pattered and the congregation took up the chant.

> "Where has my brother gone?
> Gone further on down the road!
> Where has my sister gone?
> Gone further on down the road!"

Within minutes, several Mothers began to dance jerkily, soon joined by the bearded Bishop and newly-ordained Leader Henry. As if preparing to give the Leader a piggy-back ride, the Bishop reached behind him, over his shoulders, and held the ordainee's hands. In this odd position, the pair of them danced in perfect step around the centre pole, the Bishop's elbows pointing forwards like horns.

When the dance ended, Bishop Jacob announced that Leader Henry would complete the ordination ceremony by tasting "holy water for purity."

A glass of water was produced, with white flowers in it. Leader Henry tipped the water into his mouth, without disturbing the flowers, and gargled noisily. A Mother stood by, holding a basin, into which the Leader spat. Then taking the glass from an impassive Sister, he drank the rest of the leafy water, leaving the flowers high and dry. Now he was truly a Leader.

"Let the coffin be closed", commanded Bishop Jacob.

When this had been done, the Bishop placed two silver swords, each about two feet long, side by side on the coffin lid. Granny Wilkins sighed, and that night's service drew to a close.

Thursday
Mrs. Wiltshire appeared at my door, an apparition in a huge cloak checkered in black and yellow and sprinkled with fairy glitter, a white turban on her head. Together we sailed down the road to the church, a galleon flanked by a tugboat. Few mourners were present, for the night was young. Everyone was singing mournfully as we entered.

> "Shall we all ever gather
> On that great judgment morning,
> When the trumpet sound
> And we all see Jesus?
> When the book is opened

> And my name is called,
> How sad I shall be
> When I take my departure,
> And turn my back on Heaven
> For not serving God!"

This sad, unusual song, with its quirky rhythm, was to become the theme song of Bishop Powell's funeral, along with the ubiquitous "Jordan River." Some people sang "department" instead of "departure." When the church had filled up, Mother Shepherdesses cleared the bells and candles from the lid, and the coffin was opened. Jacob, the visiting Bishop, sat in a corner, grave and silent. Mother Jewel took over as mistress of ceremonies. Red-faced, with eyes and cheeks shining, she seemed possessed of manic energy and unnatural cheerfulness, as she roared out orders in sergeant-majorish style.

"Sing louder! Sing louder, brethren, or I'll put him back to bed! (Here she made a motion towards the coffin lid, and everyone hurriedly sang louder). If you want to view, go now!"

Moving in time to the slow bongo drum rhythm, everybody filed round the coffin, gazing intently at the shrunken form of Bishop Powell. Without his flamboyant spirit, the Bishop seemed half his usual size, his full-bodied beard now reduced to grey wisps. I took my seat in the shadow of the upright coffin lid, a barn-door-like barrier. Over the top of this partition, behind the open coffin, I could see processions of waving flags, yellow and Grand Prix, moving without their bearers. Mourners took flags, as they entered from the street, and the never-ending flutter of bright colours reminded me of flocks of disorientated butterflies. At one point, Mother Jewel rushed outside into the street, where chalk spirit-writing now covered the pavement, and roared incoherently at passers-by.

"Give her my card now", Mrs. Wiltshire told me.

It seemed an inappropriate time to hand Mother Jewel a "Deepest Sympathy" card, but I did as I was told. Unable to reach her in the crowd, I gave the card to a Shepherdess who anxiously zig-zagged between flags holding up the envelope. Mother Jewel read the poem inside carefully and put the card on a shelf, to Mrs. Wiltshire's satisfaction. Then she ordered the flag-wavers to halt, and led a tiny little shy girl up to the centre pole. "This little damsel is only three year old, yet she have got a funeral song for Bishop Powell", Mother Jewel informed us.

'The poor damsel looked nervously around, whispered a few lines, then chanted aloud: "Fire gon' burn 'em! Fire gon' burn 'em!"

Everyone clapped in baffled appreciation, and Mother Jewel explained the song.

"When our dear Bishop is buried, if anyone tamper with the grave in any way, then fire is gonna burn 'em! That's what the song say - 'Fire gon' burn 'em.' If anyone does tamper, you'll know them, 'cos they'll shout 'Fire!' (Laughter). Tomorrow, brethren, when we lay

Bishop Powell to rest, don't take flowers or gifts from other people and bring them here, without you ask me first. Be wise! You know that some people try to make trouble for little Mount Pisgah!"

Bishop Jacob, the deceased's cousin, at last came forward. Everyone seemed reassured to see him there. However, he merely announced a Testimony Time, spoke a few words of praise for his cousin, and sat down once more, fingering his beard. A grim old turbaned lady, her face a crab's pincer of nose and chin, sat with her spirit-wand propped under her chin like a walking stick. Others rose to give their testimonies.

"When our dear Bishop Powell was sleeping, in his sick-bed", one tragic-eyed Mother told us, "me peep in to see him, and there is another man there, shining so! As soon as I see him, I realise - it is John the Baptist. I just stood there, an' John the Baptist turn to me with a smile and tell me not to grieve over our dear Brother. Yes, that day John the Baptist give me all kind of good advice."

Claps greeted this testimony. Leader Tony Henry, the Anancy story-man, then testified.

"One night, long before Bishop Powell die, when he was fit and well, he appeared to me in a dream and said, 'Let me show you how to look after black people.' So he show me, and here I am today, to testify of his wonderful love..."

As testimonies flowed thick and fast, a disquieting note crept in, as Mothers laughingly spoke of Bishop Powell's strictness.

" 'E take the cord to me, many a time!" one Sister testified.

"So it true, what I heard, then", Mrs. Wiltshire whispered to me.

"He take the cord from off his waist an' whip his people if they displease him. Yes!"

Testimony Time ended in wild wordless screams from several Mothers, screams that died down into prayers that were soon to be quelled by an outbreak of frantic bell-ringing over the coffin. Leader Henry produced two silver swords, held them up, then clashed them across one another, as if he were sharpening knives. He passed the swords to Bishop Jacob who solemnly laid them crossed on his cousin's body.

"That's what Rosicrucians do!" Mrs. Wiltshire told me in a pleasurably shocked undertone. "A Lodge! This whole funeral must be paid for by the Rosicrucian Lodge!"

Processions around and around the corpse began anew, with more flag-waving. Viewing the corpse seemed to be the ultimate treat for these worshippers, and there were gasps of dismay when Mother Jewel prepared to close the coffin lid once more.

"Brethren! It's your last chance to give him a cuddle!" she shouted "One quick cuddle, and I close him up for the night. I am lucky, you know! The mortuary let me have the body here in church from Monday to Friday. Normally, only kings and queens have bodies on display for that long time. The mortuary people, they took him and embalm him - they handle him like an egg! That is because they can tell he is someone special."

Bishop Jacob, Leader Henry and Mother Jewel then closed the coffin and began to beat with their palms on the lid, using it as a drum. Drumbeats formed a rhythm, and everybody sang "Roll, Jordan, Roll." Gradually, more and more people began to dance "in the spirit", until the church was rocking. Evangelist Wiltshire, enormous as she is, sailed in a trance to the middle of the floor and danced with the best of them.

At two in the morning, Leader Tony Henry closed the service with a Benediction prayer, and food and drink were brought in from the kitchen. I had a glass of bitter Mabbi, a drink made from the bark of a tree. Its bark was worse than its bite.

Friday - Burial Day.
As I entered the church for my last goodbye to Bishop Powell before he was laid in the ground, I was loudly greeted by grey-bearded Bishop Jacob. The imposing visiting Bishop wore white, a red cross adorning his white bishop's head-dress. He exuded a strong force of character and looked as if he had stepped from another century. Could
Rasputin have looked like this?
Wreaths were piled around the coffin, including one made in the shape of a bishop's hat, and another of the "Gates of Heaven."

"Jesus is knocking at the door", the people sang, then switched to proper "hymnbook hymns" from a song-sheet. Never had I seen the little church so packed. Women dressed like nuns, in white robes and head-dresses, squeezed in beside men in suits and little girls in party frocks.

Mrs. Wiltshire, a soulful yet dignified expression in her large eyes, sat a little way away from my accustomed place, behind the raised lid of the open coffin. She wore a white lace shawl over her head and shoulders, a black and white checked turban visible beneath the netting.

Bishop Jacob broke off from a eulogy on his cousin to exclaim "Welcome, Bishop George Gifford McGilvery."

A slim man with dark expressive eyes, Bishop McGilvery strode into the candle-lit darkness of the church, crowds melting before him. Clad entirely in imperial purple robes, a purple sash around his waist, he could have stepped from a gilded court of antiquity. On his head was a golden crown studded with glimmering rubies, a medieval fairy-tale come to life. I drew in my breath in wholehearted approval. Perhaps the crown and jewels would not have stood the test of bright daylight, but for me, and for most of the mourners they excelled anything on Tower Hill, and did great honour to the departed. Possibly Bishop McGilvery was a bus or train driver when he was not Bishopping - if so, this was his hour of glory.

The two living Bishops greeted one another, while the third Bishop awaited events. Bishop

Jacob, in his Crusader garb, once more began to eulogise. Suddenly he stopped.

"Here comes another Bishop!" he cried in wonder, as a cross-looking man in a black gown, floppy Elizabethan hat and dark glasses came in. This was almost too much for the congregation, who looked stunned. Supposing himself to be outranked, Bishop John politely stepped aside for the newcomer.

"Which Bishop are you?" he asked in natural curiosity, as if all London were erupting Bishops, the supply inexhaustible.

"I am Pastor Hamilton!" the pseudo-Bishop barked irritably.

Bishops Jacob and McGilvery looked a shade less respectful at this admission, but allowed the visiting pastor to make a speech.

"Now, before you have your last chance to make your earthly goodbye to our beloved Bishop Powell, Teacher Shirley will deliver a Eulogy on his life", Bishop Jacob announced.

A young woman in robes stepped forward and addressed the church in a clear, high voice.

"Bishop Powell was born in Carriacou, a little island north of Grenada, on the twelfth of June, nineteen thirty one. At the moment of his birth, his mother received a Vision. She saw a golden medal descending, inscribed with these words: 'A Gift of God.'

"Though strong and mischievous as a young man, one day young Victor Emmanuel Powell grew ill. It was a yager fever (ague) Ill and in fever for three weeks, young Victor Powell began to pray. The Angel Gabriel appeared to him in a vision and said, 'Serve God or die!'

"So at that time, Victor Emmanuel Powell made his mind up to serve God, since he decided he was too young to die. Seven serpents came out from his body, and the Angel Gabriel slew each one with a mighty sword. Then Victor Powell recovered and began to go to church and pray. But since he had been brought up an Anglican, he went to the Anglican church.

"Then one day the great Spiritual Baptist Leader named Batiste came to Carriacou from Trinidad, with all his followers. Victor Powell believed this to be heresy, so he rode out to the open-air meeting on a donkey to break it up. But when he got there, the donkey won't go, not a step! So the young man sit on the donkey and listen to Batiste
preaching instead.

"Batiste say 'I have seen a Vision of a young man destined to be a Great Leader in my church!' All at once, Victor Powell realised that the Great Leader was he himself! So full of emotion, he ran forward to tell Batiste he was here! Batiste embraced him, and took him away for preparation. He washed Victor Powell, he anointed him with olive oil, and Victor Emmanuel Powell was baptised at Dover Village. Afterwards, Batiste took our future Bishop back with him to Trinidad, where Victor Powell was taken to the Throne of Grace, the State of

The Spiritual Baptist Church

Grace arrived at by long fasting and prayer.

"From Trinidad, Victor Powell came to London to study Theology, and was consecrated as Bishop by Blessed Boltwood, whose picture you see on the wall. It was expected that Bishop Powell should only stay in London a little while and then go back to Trinidad. But in a Vision, an angel told him to remain in London, so he stayed here to be our guide and mainstay for thirty two years till Death overtook him and he was called home. Here ends my Eulogy."

To the slow mournful strains of "Shall We All Ever Gather", with tappings of bongo drums, the whole church arose and began to crocodile round and round the open coffin, each person pausing to gaze long and deeply on Bishop Powell's peaceful face. Some reached into the coffin and shook the dead man's hand. Mother Jewel picked up a tubby little girl and sat her on Bishop Powell's chest. The three year old girl looked solemn and important, as she sat partly supported by Mother Jewel's arm.

"That's Bishop Powell's own daughter", a visiting woman whispered.

"All the church pickney belong for Bishop Powell", her friend whispered back.

Mother Jewel hadn't heard this, luckily. She was busy lifting children, for each liftable child, boy or girl, had to be held over the corpse for a minute and then passed over it, to ease the passing of the Bishop's soul. No children objected, though it was easy to see that this experience didn't stand high in their list of treats. Finally, the coffin was closed. Taking a piece of chalk, Bishop Jacob began energetically to write mystic Spiritual Baptist runes on the lid.

Mother Shepherdesses lived up to their names, and shepherded us all out of the church, a great unwinding serpent of a mourning crocodile line. As we bottle-necked out of the narrow doorway, ushers holding plates stood outside to the right and left. Their optimism was largely unrewarded, although the funeral must have been a very expensive one.

Suddenly, terrible screams rent the air, for Leader Henry had nailed the lid down and Mother Jewel in horror seemed to realise her true position for the first time. No longer could she treat her dear husband's body as a doll. Now she had no husband.
Dreadful though her shrieks had been, they soon died away, and she hurried out to organise the procession to the graveyard. Everyone was milling about uncertainly. Mrs. Wiltshire appeared to be gathering gossip from Bishop Powell's adult children. Floral wreaths lay stacked against the front of the church.

"Line up three by three – what's the matter with black people?" Mother Jewel roared, a sergeant major once more.

A white van stood parked at an angle. At the sound of Mother Jewel's roar, the driver jumped out, ran round and opened the van's rear doors, to reveal a fully-set-up steel band and three dissipated-looking youths with cigarettes hanging from their mouths. Hastily disposing of these, the youths began to play very prettily, considering that they were a generation removed from Trinidad, the home of "pan."

Not from the dustbin-lid-like pans themselves, but from the low echoing roar behind the tinkling, the tune "Amazing Grace" miraculously emerged. Singing along to the tune, the mourners, Mrs. Wiltshire and I, prepared to follow the van in a great stream along the road to the Bishop's last resting place. A friendly policeman turned up, to keep order and to direct the traffic on the main road. Four pall-bearers lifted the coffin, helped by those around, and carried it out of the door. Bishop Powell had left his church for the last time.

His coffin, covered in flowers, seemed lost in the midst of the crowd. Somehow the crowd lengthened out into a procession, the coffin surrounded by flag-waving mourners. Volunteer pall-bearers helped to lighten the load, marching shoulder to shoulder. Led by the open-backed van, with the pied piper musicians inside, Mrs. Wiltshire, myself and hundreds of other mourners swept around the corner of the road into the main highway.

A group of pinch-faced Cockney men and women, probably going to or from a car-boot sale, stopped to stare in open-mouthed disapproval.

"It's not a carnival - look, they've got a coffin", one of them remarked.

Stepping out of the procession onto the pavement, so as to look at it from outside, I gazed in some awe at the lines of bobbing flags and the rows of dancing mourners. Many of the squat old ladies, brimming in health and vigour, seemed to be thoroughly enjoying themselves. With broad smiles on their broad faces, and twinkling Mrs. Tiggy Winkle eyes, they piston-danced behind the coffin, elbows jerking in and out in time to the music. Mrs. Wiltshire was among them, eyes closed in dreamy complacency, and turban bobbing. Everyone poured through the cemetery gates, leaving the main road once more free for motor traffic. With smiles, the police departed. No newspaper, local or otherwise, ever carried a photo of the remarkable scene or made mention of the funeral.

The steel band van stopped at the entrance to a narrow tree-lined lane, near the crematorium. Willing pall-bearers carried the coffin up tussocky banks, between trees and headstones, to the narrow muddy place where heaped earth indicated an open grave. There the coffin was lowered on strips of canvas to its final resting place. Crowds gathered round, as the farewell singing and preaching began. Mourners tottered unsteadily upon mud, graves and wet grass. A mournful yellow sunset streaked the sky, pierced by bare black branches.

"When white people die, dem criminate", one Mother observed to another, with a glance at the crematorium.

Bishop Powell's grave lay beneath a large overhanging willow tree, the brown twigs like bunches of thick hair. In mournful tones, the crowd began to sing an old spiritual, "No Grave Can Hold My Body Down." White-clad Bishop Jacob and purple-clad Bishop McGilvery preached in turns. Mother Jewel seemed once more aware of her bereavement, and screamed and screamed. At last she drew quiet, then Bishop McGilvery rolled white eyes up to Heaven

and fainted clean away, equally overcome by the occasion. His gorgeous bejewelled crown fell from his head and rolled away into the grass. Mourners caught the Bishop before he hit the ground, and lowered him gently down on the grass. The crown was passed from hand to hand, until it reached his head. With its restoration, he recovered, and staggered to his feet.
Young Brother Gifton, who is about fifteen, now took a spade and vigorously began to shovel earth from a heap down onto the coffin, the clods flying. Following his example, other mourners took handfuls of earth and threw them into the grave. Meanwhile, the steel band players at last called it a day, closed the van and made off. They had expected to play their way back to the church once more, but the burial service showed no sign of ending, and they had to leave.

Mrs. Wiltshire and I picked our way carefully to a dry stretch of road, where the Evangelist spoke excitedly, mixing prayers and preaching with gossip about the departed Bishop.

"I knew him was married twice, but now me hear he been married three times", she said. "He have so many children, almost all the church pickney are his own, and he get the Sisters marry off to the Brothers after he make them pregnant. Some say he have a child by his own daughter! Yes! Everyone was out to obeah him, back home and in this country, but he too smart for them till now. I wonder how he let his guard down like this? Eh, eh, this young lady his daughter by he first wife." So saying, she introduced me to a self-possessed well-dressed girl in her late twenties.

"My mother lives in America now", she told me calmly. "Yes, the Bishop is my dad, but I hadn't seen him in years. I think I'll go up now and throw earth on him, so excuse me."

Soon the grave was filled in and levelled, a wooden cross planted firmly on top.

"When we get the money, we're going to tomb him", Leader Henry told me earnestly. "We ll raise a stone or marble tomb around him and hold Remembrance Services and parades each year at this time."

Watery sunset gave way to dusk, and mourners began to drift back to the church and the Community Centre opposite. Tea, croissants and a small feast of rice and curry had been prepared by dutiful Mothers who had foregone the pleasure of the funeral for our benefit.

Traditionally, people are supposed to call their neighbours all kind of names while they're alive, and praise them once they're dead. But with Bishop Powell it was different. I had never heard a word breathed against him while he was alive, only fulsome praise. Now he was dead, everybody seemed to be criticising him, in a whispering undercurrent below the main tide of the funeral. Perhaps nobody felt safe to criticise him until he was buried and pinned down by a cross, for almost everyone thought he had supernatural powers. Regular church members have never yet "blasphemed" Bishop Powell - the murmurers were all invited guests, such as Mrs. Wiltshire.

"Had three wives, you know - Mother Jewel is his last."

The Spiritual Baptist Church

"How many children, you say?"

"No one knows even he don't know. But all the church sister dem in love with him, especially Sister Valerie Smith. When him get vex, him take off he belt and beat them, you know!"

"Yes, all o' them sister jealous o' one another, you know..."

An admirer of Bishop Powell despite his faults, Mrs. Wiltshire tried to redress the balance by telling a sister mourner of the day the Bishop had saved the Queen's life. The two old ladies sat on rickety wooden chairs facing one another in the big draughty Community Centre hall, paper plates of meat and rice balanced on their knees.

"Yes, you know Bishop Powell see in a vigion (vision) that rebels plan to assassinate the Queen of Hengland! Yes, the Queen! So he warn the Queen, and he pray and pray, till the hassassin dem grow weak, and can't lift a gun or a knife. He pray them off, and dem give up the idea altogether and the Queen get save."

"What, really? How did Bishop Powell warn the Queen?"

"In a vigion, me tell you!"

"But did the Queen get the vision?"

"No, Bishop Powell did - are you stupid? The whole thing happen in the vigion, and that prevent it happening in the natural. The Queen may never know of her narrow hescape."

Mrs. Wiltshire's companion ate her food pensively. Once so excited by this story, she now seemed to be thinking that really it wasn't much of a story at all.

When the excitement of the funeral had died down, some weeks later I attended evening service at Mount Pisgah. I found, to my disappointment, that Leader Tony Henry kept quietly in his seat. Mother Jewel, as strident as ever, was now the real church leader.
Red faced, stamping up and down, with eyes flashing, she addressed the church. Outside, violent gusts of wind and rain shook and rattled at the door. All eyes were on Mother Jewel as she ranted. Leader Tony Henry looked particularly humble. Earlier that day, I had seen him atop a ladder, screwdriver in hand, as he tried to remove the now out-of-date noticeboard above the door.

"When a sinner commit a sin, he throw himself into a precipit!" Mother Jewel shouted in mid-prowl. "No use casting out the devil if God is not in your heart! You know what happen? The devil go back, 'cause he place swept and garnished! The devil, driven out, he roams around, then he says 'At least I know my own yard' and he go back! He find it so nice, he invite all he friend in for a blues. Then you are worse than before!"

(By a 'blues', Mother Jewel meant a 'blues party', or social dance).

"Mount Pisgah Church, the devil have been active! We in Mount Pisgah have been insulted by the church in Slough! The church at Slough have declared enmity to Mount Pisgah."

Everyone gasped. In Bishop Powell's day, Mount Pisgah and the Spiritual Baptists of Slough had seemed united in brotherly love, with much to-ing and fro-ing. As Mother Jewel spoke, in Betjemanic prose, on the evils of Slough, the storm broke outside. Thunder roared, lightning burst into blue spurts of flame, and the rain came down in torrents, drumming at the door like African masqueraders demanding entrance.

"Rain come", a Brother remarked sagely.

At the next crash and hiss in the Heavens, a woman jumped up in fright.

"Sit down, Sister!" roared Mother Jewel. "I will tell you how Slough behave to little Mount Pisgah! A Sister from there come here, and she kiss me on the lips! I felt it was a Judas kiss. She gave me an invitation to her church pastor memorial service, but I say that we here in Mount Pisgah have our own pastor memorial to see to. Now I receive this invitation card by post. Read it, Sister!"

The nervous woman, glad to have something to take her mind off the lightning, took the card and read it aloud. In one corner, the woman from Slough had written: "We regret there is so little love in your church at present, but if you relent, we would still like to invite you to our late pastor's memorial service."

"They say we no go", shouted Mother Jewel, whose flashing eyes subdued the lightning outside. "But is that an invitation or an insult? It is an insult! People come to Mount Pisgah for mockery! They think we are a puppy-show! I box their ears and let them go! I let them know that I mean to rule!"

No one challenged her, so looking more than ever like the tyrant Queen of "Alice in Wonderland", she called on a fat but bent old lady to "sing out a lively chorus." Performing a bendy dance to her song, the old lady put on a vengeful anti-Slough expression and began. Gradually, others joined in.

> "My enemies are coming like a snake in the grass!
> There's one more river to cross.
> One more river to cross, and that's the River of Jordan,
> My enemies are coming like a snake in the grass,
> There's one more river to cross!"

I turned up my jacket collar, and hurried home through the rain. Above my head, it seemed as if Jehovah and Shango were battling for control of the elements.

The storm-induced hate sermon seemed to sever my friendship with Mount Pisgah, but there were other Spiritual Baptist Churches in nearby neighbourhoods. One pastor (according to rumour) had been deported by the Home Office for sacrificing a fowl at a service held in a hired Methodist hall. This incident seemed to be regarded by the church members as government persecution. Spiritual Baptists have certainly been persecuted in their country of origin, Trinidad. Between nineteen seventeen and nineteen fifty one, under British rule, the church was regarded there as an illegal organisation and officially banned. Other British-ruled islands passed similar laws.

My impression is that the British authorities had been pressed into action by the urgings of all the other Trinidadian churches. Anti-Spiritual Baptist feeling still runs high among Caribbean Pentecostalists, who fear hidden witchcraft in African-influenced churches. If Haitian "voodoo" is witchcraft, the Pentecostalists may have a point, as there are parallels between Haitian folk religion and the Spiritual Baptist faith. I know of a Haitian shrine in London where white doves are sacrificed regularly. Like most Spiritual Baptists, the Haitians have benign intentions, of worshipping God and banishing demons.

Although Mount Pisgah and Mount Ararat Spiritual Baptist Churches grow daily more African, with a Haitian flavour, many other Spiritual Baptist Churches in England are growing (or dreaming) towards Roman Catholic influences.

Prayer meetings and Bible readings in people's flats, a frequent occurrence all over West Indian Britain, carry an echo of the "early-earlies", the first-immigrant days of the nineteen fifties and sixties. Before vicars had learned to hire out their halls, and before church members could afford to buy their own premises, Caribbean churches began to take shape in front rooms, back rooms and humble homes of all kinds. One Spiritual Baptist Church, Melchisedec, still meets every week in the back room of the lady pastor's house. Seeking a change from the new harshness of Mount Pisgah, I decided to pay this church a visit.

On a snowy winter's evening, I knocked on the door of Melchisedec and was shown through to the back room by a sprightly and un-churchy young man of the house. The charming little terraced house, which adjoined an archway leading to a cobbled mews-turned garage, was home to a large boisterous West Indian family. Few of them attended the church in their own house. Melchisedec was pastored by a frail blue-turbaned grandmother, Mother Burris. My friend Evangelist Wiltshire had told me of this church.

"You are no stranger, but a friend of Mother Wiltshire", Mother Burris smiled through her spectacles.

The room was crowded with big, beaming, friendly Grenadans and Trinidadians. Gingerly I found one empty chair, sat down and took a look around. Most of the members wore white robes. A Iota, or golden ball-vase, gleamed on the altar table, and a cross within a circle had been scratched into the wall, as in a Dark Age Celtic church. A slender woman in scarlet robes rang a handbell, and Bible-reading began, followed by music from hand-claps and a calabash strung all over with rattling beads.

' Jesus rode on the water so bright!" Mother Burris carolled in a high but unquavering voice.

A bearded man in white became affected by the Holy Spirit. He and two Sisters in turbans began a lunging dance, their elbows jerking in and out like pistons. Although the small room was crowded, no one was poked and no candles were knocked over.

When the song was over, and people had calmed down, a stout motherly woman read out the Announcements. There would be a coach excursion to Our Lady's Shrine at Walsingham, and another to a Friary in the country, where they had been given permission to hold a service. A boy of eight began to talk to a dainty little girl who sat nearby, to the rage of one of the turbaned women. She seized him by one arm and hurled him violently across the room, where he sat on a stool weeping silently.

"Forgive him, Lord, he is only a child", the Announcing Sister remarked.

"Amen", said Mother Burris from her stately corner.

Taking a Bible but not opening it, the woman in scarlet warned us of the dangers of Temptation from the Adversary. I could tell that it would have seemed mildly unlucky if anyone had boldly used the Adversary's real name, Satan or Devil.

"The Adversary appeared to Adam as a beautiful virgin", she continued. "She said, 'I am Eve's sister, come lie with me.' But God protected Adam from the Adversary."

A Voice: "Praise the Lord!"

I wondered where she had learned this story. A "Novena" was then held, and I was told to hold a burning candle as I and the others prayed for our Needs, repeating the words from a Roman Catholic prayer-book. Afterwards biscuits were passed round. Younger members spoke in jolly Cockney accents, and I was made very much at home. By dint of drawing pictures in my notebook, I cheered up the eight year old boy. Outside the snow had stopped falling and London seemed as white as a Melchisedec robe.

Melchisedec's sister church is known as Mount Paran Spiritual Baptist Church. Regal women in turbans, with gowns of red, black or white, hold meetings in a hired church and in one another's flats. My sister Zenga invited the elders of the church to her own newly-acquired flat for a Caribbean-style house blessing. Their arrival was greeted with great excitement by my three year old niece, Zenga's daughter Omalara. In fact, Omalara proceeded to satirise the ceremony by trying to turn the hand-holding circle of prayer into the Hokey Cokey.

Despite this impishness, it was a moving ceremony. The leading Spiritual Mother called for a lit candle and a glass of water. Taking these, she began to sing in a rich, beautiful voice. "Hold to God's Unchanging Hand." The prayer that followed called on God as the "Lord of Africa" for to this West Indian church, Africa, Zion and Heaven are as one.

"Lord of Africa, remember your children, the poor and unhappy all over the world. Lord, we call your blessings down on such as these....."

Then she turned to the Bible, and Omalara scampered out of the room. There was a loud crash offstage, and the child returned with a heavy encyclopaedia which she held upside down and loudly pretended to read. Sister Grace scattered a few drops of water around the room, and Omalara emptied a packet of porridge oats over me.

Smiling indulgently, the Spiritual Mothers arose, the leader ringing a handbell above her head, to Omalara's delight. Then the five women walked in solemn procession up and down the large ground floor flat, reading aloud from the Twenty Fourth and Twenty Fifth Psalms. In every room, water was scattered in each corner, the bell was rung and blessings were uttered. Soon the flat seemed thoroughly blessed. Zenga gave a donation to Mount Paran, and the leading Mother abruptly changed gears, put on her Community Worker's hat and asked us to sign a petition calling for better street lighting.

Later, I bought Omalara a small handbell, so that she too could bless her home. It is blessed by her presence anyway.

Embroidered altar banner of yellow snake in central position
(Sketch by Roy Kerridge)

THE WORLD'S WEIRDEST PUBLISHING COMPANY

HOW TO START A PUBLISHING EMPIRE

Unlike most mainstream publishers, we have a non-commercial remit, and our mission statement claims that "we publish books because they deserve to be published, not because we think that we can make money out of them". Our motto is the Latin Tag *Pro bona causa facimus* (we do it for good reason), a slogan taken from a children's book *The Case of the Silver Egg* by the late Desmond Skirrow.

WIKIPEDIA: "The first book published was in 1988. *Take this Brother may it Serve you Well* was a guide to Beatles bootlegs by Jonathan Downes. It sold quite well, but was hampered by very poor production values, being photocopied, and held together by a plastic clip binder. In 1988 A5 clip binders were hard to get hold of, so the publishers took A4 binders and cut them in half with a hacksaw. It now reaches surprisingly high prices second hand.

The production quality improved slightly over the years, and after 1999 all the books produced were ringbound with laminated colour covers. In 2004, however, they signed an agreement with Lightning Source, and all books are now produced perfect bound, with full colour covers."

Until 2010 all our books, the majority of which are/were on the subject of mystery animals and allied disciplines, were published by `CFZ Press`, the publishing arm of the Centre for Fortean Zoology (CFZ), and we urged our readers and followers to draw a discreet veil over the books that we published that were completely off topic to the CFZ.

However, in 2010 we decided that enough was enough and launched a second imprint, `Fortean Words` which aims to cover a wide range of non animal-related esoteric subjects. Other imprints will be launched as and when we feel like it, however the basic ethos of the company remains the same: Our job is to publish books and magazines that we feel are worth publishing, whether or not they are going to sell. Money is, after all - as my dear old Mama once told me - a rather vulgar subject, and she would be rolling in her grave if she thought that her eldest son was somehow in `trade`.

Luckily, so far our tastes have turned out not to be that rarified after all, and we have sold far more books than anyone ever thought that we would, so there is a moral in here somewhere…

Jon Downes,
Woolsery, North Devon
July 2010

Other Books in Print

Sea Serpent Carcasses - Scotland from the Stronsa Monster to Loch Ness by Glen Vaudrey
The CFZ Yearbook 2012 edited by Jonathan and Corinna Downes
ORANG PENDEK: Sumatra's Forgotten Ape by Richard Freeman
THE MYSTERY ANIMALS OF THE BRITISH ISLES: London by Neil Arnold
CFZ EXPEDITION REPORT: India 2010 by Richard Freeman *et al*
The Cryptid Creatures of Florida by Scott Marlow
Dead of Night by Lee Walker
The Mystery Animals of the British Isles: The Northern Isles by Glen Vaudrey
THE MYSTERY ANIMALS OF THE BRTISH ISLES: Gloucestershire and Worcestershire by Paul Williams
When Bigfoot Attacks by Michael Newton
Weird Waters – The Mystery Animals of Scandinavia: Lake and Sea Monsters by Lars Thomas
The Inhumanoids by Barton Nunnelly
Monstrum! A Wizard's Tale by Tony "Doc" Shiels
CFZ Yearbook 2011 edited by Jonathan Downes
Karl Shuker's Alien Zoo by Shuker, Dr Karl P.N
Tetrapod Zoology Book One by Naish, Dr Darren
The Mystery Animals of Ireland by Gary Cunningham and Ronan Coghlan
Monsters of Texas by Gerhard, Ken
The Great Yokai Encyclopaedia by Freeman, Richard
NEW HORIZONS: Animals & Men *issues 16-20 Collected Editions Vol. 4* by Downes, Jonathan
A Daintree Diary -
Tales from Travels to the Daintree Rainforest in tropical north Queensland, Australia by Portman, Carl
Strangely Strange but Oddly Normal by Roberts, Andy
Centre for Fortean Zoology Yearbook 2010 by Downes, Jonathan
Predator Deathmatch by Molloy, Nick
Star Steeds and other Dreams by Shuker, Karl
CHINA: A Yellow Peril? by Muirhead, Richard
Mystery Animals of the British Isles: The Western Isles by Vaudrey, Glen
Giant Snakes - Unravelling the coils of mystery by Newton, Michael

Mystery Animals of the British Isles: Kent by Arnold, Neil
Centre for Fortean Zoology Yearbook 2009 by Downes, Jonathan
CFZ EXPEDITION REPORT: Russia 2008 by Richard Freeman *et al*, Shuker, Karl (fwd)
Dinosaurs and other Prehistoric Animals on Stamps - A Worldwide catalogue by Shuker, Karl P. N
Dr Shuker's Casebook by Shuker, Karl P.N
The Island of Paradise - chupacabra UFO crash retrievals, and accelerated evolution on the island of Puerto Rico by Downes, Jonathan
The Mystery Animals of the British Isles: Northumberland and Tyneside by Hallowell, Michael J
Centre for Fortean Zoology Yearbook 1997 by Downes, Jonathan (Ed)
Centre for Fortean Zoology Yearbook 2002 by Downes, Jonathan (Ed)
Centre for Fortean Zoology Yearbook 2000/1 by Downes, Jonathan (Ed)
Centre for Fortean Zoology Yearbook 1998 by Downes, Jonathan (Ed)
Centre for Fortean Zoology Yearbook 2003 by Downes, Jonathan (Ed)
In the wake of Bernard Heuvelmans by Woodley, Michael A
CFZ EXPEDITION REPORT: Guyana 2007 by Richard Freeman *et al*, Shuker, Karl (fwd)
Centre for Fortean Zoology Yearbook 1999 by Downes, Jonathan (Ed)
Big Cats in Britain Yearbook 2008 by Fraser, Mark (Ed)
Centre for Fortean Zoology Yearbook 1996 by Downes, Jonathan (Ed)
THE CALL OF THE WILD - Animals & Men issues 11-15
Collected Editions Vol. 3 by Downes, Jonathan (ed)
Ethna's Journal by Downes, C N
Centre for Fortean Zoology Yearbook 2008 by Downes, J (Ed)
DARK DORSET -Calendar Custome by Newland, Robert J
Extraordinary Animals Revisited by Shuker, Karl
MAN-MONKEY - In Search of the British Bigfoot by Redfern, Nick
Dark Dorset Tales of Mystery, Wonder and Terror by Newland, Robert J and Mark North
Big Cats Loose in Britain by Matthews, Marcus
MONSTER! - The A-Z of Zooform Phenomena by Arnold, Neil
The Centre for Fortean Zoology 2004 Yearbook by Downes, Jonathan (Ed)
The Centre for Fortean Zoology 2007 Yearbook by Downes, Jonathan (Ed)
CAT FLAPS! Northern Mystery Cats by Roberts, Andy
Big Cats in Britain Yearbook 2007 by Fraser, Mark (Ed)
BIG BIRD! - Modern sightings of Flying Monsters by Gerhard, Ken
THE NUMBER OF THE BEAST - Animals & Men issues 6-10
Collected Editions Vol. 1 by Downes, Jonathan (Ed)
IN THE BEGINNING - Animals & Men *issues 1-5 Collected Editions Vol. 1* by Downes, Jonathan
STRENGTH THROUGH KOI - They saved Hitler's Koi and other stories by Downes, Jonathan
The Smaller Mystery Carnivores of the Westcountry by Downes, Jonathan
CFZ EXPEDITION REPORT: Gambia 2006 by Richard Freeman *et al*, Shuker, Karl (fwd)
The Owlman and Others by Jonathan Downes
The Blackdown Mystery by Downes, Jonathan
Big Cats in Britain Yearbook 2006 by Fraser, Mark (Ed)

Fragrant Harbours - Distant Rivers by Downes, John T
Only Fools and Goatsuckers by Downes, Jonathan
Monster of the Mere by Jonathan Downes
Dragons:More than a Myth by Freeman, Richard Alan
Granfer's Bible Stories by Downes, John Tweddell
Monster Hunter by Downes, Jonathan

CFZ Classics is a new venture for us. There are many seminal works that are either unavailable today, or not available with the production values which we would like to see. So, following the old adage that if you want to get something done do it yourself, this is exactly what we have done.

Desiderius Erasmus Roterodamus (b. October 18th 1466, d. July 2nd 1536) said: "When I have a little money, I buy books; and if I have any left, I buy food and clothes," and we are much the same. Only, we are in the lucky position of being able to share our books with the wider world. CFZ Classics is a conduit through which we cannot just re-issue titles which we feel still have much to offer the cryptozoological and Fortean research communities of the 21st Century, but we are adding footnotes, supplementary essays, and other material where we deem it appropriate.

Headhunters of The Amazon by Fritz W Up de Graff (1902)

Fortean Words

The Centre for Fortean Zoology has for several years led the field in Fortean publishing. CFZ Press is the only publishing company specialising in books on monsters and mystery animals. CFZ Press has published more books on this subject than any other company in history and has attracted such well known authors as Andy Roberts, Nick Redfern, Michael Newton, Dr Karl Shuker, Neil Arnold, Dr Darren Naish, Jon Downes, Ken Gerhard and Richard Freeman.

Now CFZ Press are launching a new imprint. Fortean Words is a new line of books dealing with Fortean subjects other than cryptozoology, which is - after all - the subject the CFZ are best known for. Fortean Words is being launched with a spectacular multi-volume series called *Haunted Skies* which covers British UFO sightings between 1940 and 2010. Former policeman John Hanson and his long-suffering partner Dawn Holloway have compiled a peerless library of sighting reports, many that have not been made public before.

Other books include a look at the Berwyn Mountains UFO case by renowned Fortean Andy Roberts and a series of forthcoming books by transatlantic researcher Nick Redfern. CFZ Press are dedicated to maintaining the fine quality of their works with Fortean Words. New authors tackling new subjects will always be encouraged, and we hope that our books will continue to be as ground-breaking and popular as ever.

Haunted Skies Volume One 1940-1959 by John Hanson and Dawn Holloway
Haunted Skies Volume Two 1960-1965 by John Hanson and Dawn Holloway
Haunted Skies Volume Three 1965-1967 by John Hanson and Dawn Holloway
Haunted Skies Volume Four 1968-1971 by John Hanson and Dawn Holloway
Haunted Skies Volume Five 1972-1974 by John Hanson and Dawn Holloway
Haunted Skies Volume Six 1975-1977 by John Hanson and Dawn Holloway
Grave Concerns by Kai Roberts

Police and the Paranormal by Andy Owens
Dead of Night by Lee Walker
Space Girl Dead on Spaghetti Junction - an anthology by Nick Redfern
I Fort the Lore - an anthology by Paul Screeton
UFO Down - the Berwyn Mountains UFO Crash by Andy Roberts
The Grail by Ronan Coghlan
UFO Warminster - Cradle of Contract by Kevin Goodman
Quest for the Hexham Heads by Paul Screeton

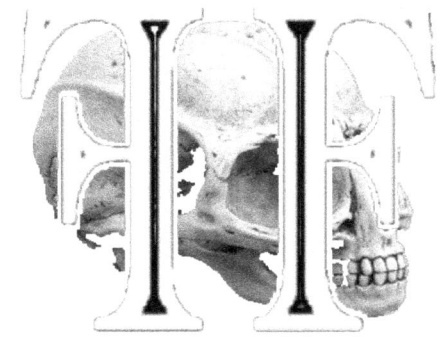

Fortean Fiction

Just before Christmas 2011, we launched our third imprint, this time dedicated to - let's see if you guessed it from the title - fictional books with a Fortean or cryptozoological theme. We have published a few fictional books in the past, but now think that because of our rising reputation as publishers of quality Forteana, that a dedicated fiction imprint was the order of the day.

We launched with four titles:

Green Unpleasant Land by Richard Freeman
Left Behind by Harriet Wadham
Dark Ness by Tabitca Cope
Snap! By Steven Bredice
Death on Dartmoor by Di Francis
Dark Wear by Tabitca Cope

www.ingramcontent.com/pod-product-compliance
Lightning Source LLC
Chambersburg PA
CBHW061342040426
42444CB00011B/3053